DYI

DYING TO LIVE

DEREK BALDWIN

eagle
Guildford, Surrey

Copyright © 1995 Derek Baldwin

The right of Derek Baldwin to be identified as author of this work has been asserted by him in accordance with the Copyright, Design and Patents Act 1988.

British Library Cataloguing in Publication Data. A catalogue record for this book is available from the British Library.

Published by Eagle, an imprint of Inter Publishing Service (IPS) Ltd, St Nicholas House, 14 The Mount, Guildford, Surrey GU2 5HN.

All rights reserved. No part of this publication may be reproduced or transmitted in any form or by any means, electronic or mechanical, including photocopying, recording or any information storage and retrieval system, without either prior permission in writing from the publisher or a licence permitting restricted copying.

In the United Kingdom such licences are issued by the Publishers Licensing Society Ltd, 90 Tottenham Court Road, London W1P 9HE.

All Scripture quotations, unless otherwise noted, are taken from the *Holy Bible, New International Version*. Copyright © 1973, 1978, 1984 by the International Bible Society. Used by permission of Hodder & Stoughton, a Division of Hodder Headline.

Other Scripture quotations are as follows:
RSV: Revised Standard Version
KJV: King James Version
Phillips: J.B. Phillips

Typeset by Palimpsest Book Production Limited, Polmont, Stirlingshire
Printed by HarperCollins

ISBN No: 0 86347 181 1

CONTENTS

Foreword by Bishop Michael Marshall	1
Introduction	3
Prologue: Sacrifice . . . ? You Can't Mean Me!	11
1. The Call to Sacrifice	14
2. The Context of Sacrifice	33
3. Church Life – (1) The Sacrificial Pattern	55
4. Church Life – (2) Worship	68
5. Church Life – (3) Relationships	86
6. Church Life – (4) Outreach	105
7. Church Life – (5) Leadership	125
8. Marriage – Made in Heaven	139
9. Family Life – Training in Discipleship	163
10. Lifestyle and Community	185
11. Dying to Self – The Big Issue	211
Epilogue	235
Notes	237

ACKNOWLEDGEMENTS

A number of people have given time and thought to reading parts of my manuscript. To all who have offered encouragement, suggestions, criticism or reproof . . . many thanks. I am extremely grateful for it all.

Particular thanks must go to two very special friends. First, to Gwenda Lewis, without whose timely reminders this would have been a less compassionate book than I hope it is. More than once she has pulled me back from the brink of being thoughtless or insensitive. Secondly, to Vernon Wilkins, who over the months has gone not just the extra mile but an extra five, painstakingly commenting on the drafts of every chapter. His comments and criticisms, always constructive and thought-provoking, have made this a much better book than it would otherwise have been.

Finally, thanks to David Wavre of Eagle Books for his encouragement and flexibility.

July 1995

*I have been crucified with Christ . . .
I live by faith in the Son of God,
who loved me and gave himself for me.*
                              Galatians 2:20

*For this is Love's prerogative –
To give – and give – and give.*
                              John Oxenham

FOREWORD

For far too long there has been a less-than-scriptural commendation of the Gospel of Christ, in terms of therapy or even entertainment, in which self-fulfilment and the 'feel-good' factor have been marketed as the goal of life. 'When the desire for self-fulfilment' writes Derek Baldwin 'becomes the magnetic north by which we navigate, our Christianity has become what I can best describe as earth-bound'.

In the kingdoms and empires of this world, it is so often a matter of every man for himself; the survival of the fittest and the law of the jungle. That is in stark contrast with the life-style of God's Kingdom in which it is always essentially a matter of life lived for others. Such a life-style is the key to that abundant quality of life that Christ holds out to us in the Gospels, both in his teaching and in his whole way of life. Interdependence replaces individualism and complementarity replaces competitive self-sufficiency. And all this because our trinitarian God has revealed himself as persons in community, giving and receiving love, within love.

Jesus shows us God's way of being truly human in a way of life which is life lived for others — what the Scriptures call the priestly way of life, in which intercession, sacrifice and prayer are central. For intercession is much more than a way of praying for others: it involves living for others and so following in the footsteps of Jesus Christ our Great High Priest who lived and died for all and who now ever lives to make intercession for us (Hebrews 7:25). So Derek Baldwin writes in this timely, challenging and disturbing book – 'self-sacrifice is the first step on a pathway of unspeakable privilege which leads to a destiny of unimaginable glory'. Our world desperately needs to hear this message which is so central and crucial for its salvation, survival and health.

Bishop Michael Marshall
Adviser in Evangelism to the Archbishops
of Canterbury and York
17 October 1995

INTRODUCTION

This is a book I did not really want to write, and may well turn out to be one you do not particularly want to read! This sounds like an exercise in utter futility. So let me explain.

The longer I live as a member of God's family, the Church, the more convinced I become that in these last decades of the twentieth century we have a serious problem with sacrifice. When I have mentioned to Christian friends that it would be the subject of this book, most found it hard to envisage what it would be about. Perhaps it is not too surprising that their minds went immediately to money and possessions; but it *is* surprising – and worrying – that so many seemed reluctant, or unable, to think beyond that. When I tried to explain that I was writing about the need for a sacrificial attitude to permeate the whole of life, I got some blank looks.

This led me to two conclusions. First, there certainly is a need to rekindle awareness of this fundamental aspect of discipleship. That encouraged me to press on with this book. Secondly, if I had found such difficulty in conveying the essence of the subject, then writing about it in an accessible and convincing way would be very hard. This tempted me to run away and leave the task for someone else far better qualified to do it! But by now the whole subject had so burned itself into my mind that escape was no longer a serious option.

* * *

As I write these words during 1995, our politicians and media are talking endlessly about the 'feel-good factor'. Because key economic statistics are not as bad as they were, we are all supposed to be full of *joie de vivre* and confidence for the future. But, to their great frustration, the polls show that we are not. Beneath all this – unspoken and largely unchallenged – lies one of the main assumptions which shape the philosophy of life today (even for those who did not know they had one!). That is the belief that we are *entitled* to feel good . . . as if this were some kind of basic human right.

Inevitably, Christians have always been influenced to some extent by the circumstances and values of their generation. But recent years have seen a communications explosion and dramatic growth in the power of the media through which pundits of all kinds bombard us with their ideas. This vastly increases the ability of the few to shape the attitudes of the many. There is a hidden danger here for Christians. We can easily absorb what we hear without considering the underlying assumptions. Then those assumptions begin (mostly unconsciously) to colour our own thinking about our lives as individuals and members of God's Church. When that happens we are in trouble, because the specific call to us is *not* to think like the world:

> Do not conform any longer to the pattern

Introduction

> of this world, but be transformed by the renewing of your mind. Then you will be able to test and approve what God's will is – his good, pleasing and perfect will.
>
> (Rom 12:2)

This uncritical absorption by Christians of the world's values has certainly happened with the 'feel-good' factor. Before you protest, let me agree right away that Christians, of all people, have reason to feel good. What could be better than to know that our lives, here and hereafter, are in the hands of an all-powerful, all-loving God – that (as Julian of Norwich said centuries ago) 'all shall be well'? In that sense, feeling good *is* a basic Christian right . . . though even then not a 'right' we deserve or have earned, but one which has been bought for us through the grace of God in sending his Son to die for us.

Moreover we can, and should, know this joy and confidence now in this life. But here we need to draw a sharp distinction.

Asserting that God wills everything to contribute to our ultimate good (Rom 8:28) is not at all the same thing as saying that to have a good time (materially and spiritually) is the main purpose of our lives, or that self-fulfilment should be their main aim.

Furthermore, the Bible nowhere teaches us that life will be a bed of roses, nor that because we are Christians we can expect – much less are entitled to – health, wealth and happiness. I do not want to be misunderstood here. Many of the current emphases in Christian living and teaching are positive and good – maybe a necessary corrective to some negative and life-denying attitudes of the past. But, looking around today, I cannot help concluding that many Christians have bought the line that self-fulfilment is the main aim of life. Then the concept of self-sacrifice as the basis for Christian living gets forgotten, obscured, or possibly even rejected. I see many signs that this is happening – hence my conviction about the need for such a book as this.

When the desire for self-fulfilment becomes the magnetic north by which we navigate, our Christianity has become what I can best describe as 'earthbound'. We may *believe* that this life is followed by a new life beyond the grave; but the way we think and behave suggests we do not see the connection between the two. The idea that our earthly life is no more nor less than a preparation for the life to come does not sound very 1990s; but it is an essential part of God's revealed truth about our relationship with him and his purpose for us. I shall return to this several times in the course of this book. I am bound to, because the only way to make any sense of the things that happen in this world – particularly those involving suffering and sacrifice – is to see them in the light of God's ultimate purpose of making us 'like Christ'. Lose that perspective, and we are in real danger of going astray. However 'fulfilled' we may think we are, we shall sooner or later come face to face with the truth of Paul's words: 'If only for this life we have hope in Christ, we are to be pitied more than all men' (1 Cor 15:19).

* * *

Introduction

Down the years many books have been written about sacrifice. The last decade has seen a new upsurge of attention to the subject among theologians. The looming environmental crisis has forced even academics and scientists to recognise on a humanistic level the need for a degree of self-denial if we are to survive . . . and that idea is feeding through via the media into popular consciousness. In the midst of all this, it is ironical that 'ordinary Christians' seem to have lost sight of this fundamental part of the faith.

Two books, in particular, have greatly affected my own thinking. Strangely, I had not read either of them when I undertook to write this book; but studying them since then has made a profound impression on me. I ought therefore to acknowledge my debt to them here since, as well as the direct quotations which I have included, I am sure there are many other places where what I have written reflects their influence.

The first is *The Cost of Discipleship* by the German theologian and pastor Dietrich Bonhoeffer.[1] After repeatedly denouncing the utter godlessness of Nazism, he was eventually arrested in 1943, spending the next two years in prison and concentration camps. Stories abound of the ways in which his towering personality and invincible faith were an immense inspiration to other prisoners. He finally paid the price for his unswerving faithfulness to his Lord, being executed in 1945 on the personal instructions of Himmler. Most of us will not have experienced anything like the test of faith which he faced. In spite of this, and of the different social and political order of our own times, I believe Bonhoeffer speaks to us very directly, sounding a clear and timely warning about the shallowness of much that passes for discipleship today.

> Discipleship means adherence to Christ . . . Christianity without the living Christ is inevitably Christianity without discipleship, and Christianity without discipleship is always Christianity without Christ. It remains an abstract idea, a myth which has a place for the Fatherhood of God, but omits Christ as the living Son . . . Discipleship without Jesus Christ is a way of our own choosing.[2]

The second is a very recent book, *The Power of Sacrifice* by Ian Bradley, a Church of Scotland minister, lecturer and broadcaster.[3] An academic book which considers the concept of sacrifice in a broad religious and historical context, and in the light of modern scientific understanding of the world, it also has a sharp cutting edge in its application to life today.

Both books make considerable demands on the reader — Bonhoeffer's by the uncompromising severity of its message, and Bradley's by the academic breadth and depth of its perspective. The present book, in a sense, begins where they leave off. My aim has been to approach the subject in a down-to-earth, practical way which will stimulate the 'person-in-the-pew' to re-examine their attitude to, and experience of, being a follower of Jesus Christ in the modern world.

But, while I hope this book will not be judged 'severe', I cannot promise that it will be an easy read. It cannot be, because (as Ian Bradley says of his book) 'its subject matter is uncongenial and more than a little forbidding'.[4] Likewise, although

Introduction

it makes no pretensions to be a work of academic theology, it must, before addressing the nitty-gritty everyday issues in what I hope is a helpful way, look again at Christ's call to all who are serious about being disciples to deny ourselves, take up our cross and follow him. Accordingly, my first two chapters seek to establish this as a common point of reference. I have tried very hard not to make them too heavy-going; but I appreciate that some readers may find these introductory chapters challenging. Please do not be tempted to skip over them on this account, because it is on these basic foundations that all the more personal and practical parts of the book depend – and we all know what happens if you try to build a house without foundations!

From Chapter Three onwards we examine some of the areas of life where the principle of self-sacrifice must be applied. Although these chapters are more practical, they are no less challenging. In order not to get discouraged, or 'turned off' altogether, we shall need to remember constantly that this kind of living *can* be achieved – but only through the power of the Holy Spirit whom God gives to every Christian.

Most of the areas we look at have both an individual and a corporate dimension, with a need to look both inward and outward. There is a constant ebb and flow between the two; they are never very far apart, and in practice they often have a profound effect on each other. The last chapter tries to pull some of the strands together, asking how far the final citadel of self has been yielded to Christ. Even here, as we look into the innermost recesses of our conscious selves, we also look away to Christ, and to the totally loving nature of his invasion of our lives.

It is my prayer that, as we consider together the call of Christ to follow him along the way of self-sacrifice, we shall hear and understand afresh his own words to us:

> For whoever wants to save his life will lose it, but whoever loses his life for me will find it.
> (Matt 16:25)

PROLOGUE

SACRIFICE...? YOU CAN'T MEAN ME!

'Yes – you're quite right, of course. Christians are supposed to make sacrifices. I accept that. But if you could see *my* problems . . . if you knew what I'm going through. That's about all I need right now, someone starting to lecture *me* about sacrifice. It's the last straw. You can't mean me!'

I can imagine that will be some people's reaction to this book. I know that some readers will have relationship problems, marriages breaking up or ended, traumas with children or elderly parents – others will have been bereaved, or wake up each day worrying about finances or losing their job. For some, church life may be far from satisfactory, bringing tension or frustration rather than encouragement and fellowship. The list is endless – and some will have problems I cannot even imagine. Nobody's life is completely free from anxiety and suffering. As a wise man wrote several thousand years ago: 'Man is born to trouble as surely as sparks fly upward' (Job 5:7). But it seems so unfair. Some people seem to sail through life, while others have far more than their share of trouble. As soon as one agonising problem is out of the way another comes hard on its heels.

Christians can find this very hard to understand or accept. It may cause them to question God's love. At such times even well-meaning advice about how God allows trouble in our lives to deepen our trust and make us grow in patience and perseverance can seem hollow – let alone someone coming along and telling them they must take up their cross, be less self-centred . . .

As I have worked on this book, I have repeatedly been stopped in my tracks, realising that what I have just written might seem harsh or insensitive. It could easily be misunderstood; it might discourage, upset or cause real personal hurt or distress. Nothing could be further from my intentions. This has been the hardest problem I have had to face.

- Should I hedge every point about with countless provisos and apologies, to show that I appreciate all the traumas readers might be experiencing? This would soon get tedious – and make a very long book!
- Should I avoid altogether any statements which, whilst issuing a needed challenge to one reader, might be inappropriate or even upsetting to another? That would risk defeating the purpose of writing the book at all; and I cannot afford to run that risk, since I believe there *is* an urgently-needed message here.
- Should I print a 'health warning' suggesting that those going through stress or hardship had better not read the book at all? I quickly abandoned this, convinced as I am that God calls *all* his children to live sacrificially – including those whose lives are full of unhappiness and pain.

In the end I concluded that I could only press on, making every effort to be loving and sensitive, but ultimately trusting the Holy Spirit to use my words to convict and challenge without causing unnecessary hurt or harm. It is with that prayer that I have undertaken this work.

* * *

To assert that the way of the Cross is the only true way of discipleship is not, in fact, a negative message, but a positive one. The way of self-sacrifice which God sets before us is not a burden he lays on us, but a privilege he offers us. In following it we may gain a greater awareness of his sacrificial love than in any other way, and at the same time find our own capacity for love deepened.[1] Whatever God may be asking you to bear, you have only to look at the Cross to know that *he* is not hard-hearted. Please believe that neither am I. Wherever my words may strike you as inappropriate or too demanding, please remember that although I do not know your personal circumstances, God does. Seek to hear what *he* may be saying to you about sacrifice even in the midst of them.

> Therefore we do not lose heart. Though outwardly we are wasting away, yet inwardly we are being renewed day by day. For our light and momentary troubles are achieving for us an eternal glory that far outweighs them all. So we fix our eyes not on what is seen, but on what is unseen. For what is seen is temporary, but what is unseen is eternal.
> (2 Cor 4:16–18)

ONE
THE CALL TO SACRIFICE

Then [Jesus] said to them all: 'If anyone would come after me, he must deny himself and take up his cross daily and follow me.'
(Luke 9:23)

The life of constant self-denial is the life of constant assent to God.
(William Barclay)[1]

If we were to be asked whether we take the words of Jesus seriously, I imagine most of us who call ourselves Christians would say we do – or, at any rate, we certainly try to. So what about the words at the head of this chapter – one of the most important and most challenging of the recorded sayings of Jesus? They are, of course, familiar; at the very least we usually take them out and inspect them, and maybe think seriously about them, during Lent. And then what . . . ?

But look at them again, carefully and prayerfully (and outside the context of giving up chocolate and being nice to people!) and it will be immediately apparent that they have the potential to turn our personal world completely upside down. Not only that, but there is no way of escaping them. Just consider:

The Call to Sacrifice

If *anyone* would come after me . . . that leaves no room for suggesting that what Jesus is saying applies only to certain people – monks and nuns, missionaries or those with a special vocation.

He *must* deny himself and take up his cross . . . no scope there for thinking this self-denial is optional, something we can choose to do or not do according to our point of view, or how 'religious' we are inclined to be.

. . . deny himself and take up his cross *daily* and follow me . . . so this is not something we can take up for a period, like Lent or in preparation for some special event in our lives, and then go back to 'normal' afterwards.

There is no straightforward, honest interpretation of this command which allows us to wriggle out of it. It's not just for some Christians, but includes us all. It's not a maybe, but a must. It's not just when I feel like it, but all the time. It is the very definition of what it means to be a disciple of Christ – the Founder's own manifesto for the way of life of all who want to follow him. And perhaps the most significant words of all are the final ones – '*and follow me*'. By his own way of life and death, Jesus Christ has provided us with a startlingly clear example of what he meant. That firmly closes the final loophole that we might try to wriggle through – that we do not really know what following him means.

In short, the truly Christian life is one of total self-sacrifice. Anything less falls short of the call that Christ himself issued and the pattern that he himself set.

Two things strike me immediately about that statement:

> It is not only immensely challenging, but also utterly humbling. It cuts us down to size; it shows up our best attempt at discipleship for the poor and inadequate thing that it is; it brings us face to face with our tendency to pick and choose amongst the sayings of Jesus for those we find most 'convenient'.
>
> Self-sacrifice is totally opposite to the way most people see life.

Those two things are connected: even as Christians we find the demand for self-sacrifice uncongenial because, however much we may like to believe otherwise, we are constantly influenced by the way the world thinks. The extent to which the world's unspoken (and often unchallenged) assumptions have penetrated the thinking of individual Christians and congregations is a main theme of this book. We are called to be '*transformed* by the renewing of our minds' – the very opposite of being *conformed* to the pattern of the world's way of thinking (Rom 12:2). And we are not left without information about what we are to be transformed into – the likeness (or image) of Christ (Rom 8:29). That image holds out the ultimate promise of unimaginable glory; but its immediate significance is the call to a life of sacrifice, for the image of Christ's earthly life is, above all, one of total self-giving love. In this fundamental of Christian discipleship, there is a good deal of 'conforming' to be repented of, and much 'transforming' to be undertaken, in our approach to Christian living today.

The Origin of Self-Centredness

It will therefore be instructive to look at the context in which Jesus issued this call to follow him – particularly in the slightly fuller version which appears in Matthew 16:21–26. Jesus had been telling his disciples about the testing events that lay ahead. He knew that they would prove so horrifying that his followers were likely – as proved to be the case – to be completely thrown by them. And so he did his best to prepare his friends, telling them about his coming suffering, death and resurrection. Peter, acting as their spokesman, immediately homed in on the suffering and death and seems to have ignored the bit about resurrection. (We shall explore this tendency more fully in the next chapter.) Speaking off the top of his head, as he so often did, he said, 'No, Lord. Never! We love you . . . we can't have this sort of thing happening to you!' Impetuous it may have been, but his reaction was utterly genuine and well-intentioned, what any friend worth the name would have done. Most of us would probably have reacted in the same way if we had been there. Yet it brought from Jesus one of the most forthright and apparently scathing retorts we read anywhere in the Gospels. What caused this strong reaction, and what does it have to say to us?

First, Peter's words must have been such a disappointment to Jesus. Immediately before this episode Matthew records Peter's great confession, 'You are the Christ, the Son of the living God', evoking Christ's reply, 'This was not revealed to you by man, but by my Father in heaven.' Now the situation is turned on its head. Peter says, in effect, 'No, Lord, we can't have you suffering; if this is going to be the cost of doing the work you were anointed to do [Christ = the anointed one] we must try to find some other way.' It amounts to a denial of his earlier confession, and as such it produces from Jesus an opposite response: whereas the confession was 'not revealed to you by man', its denial shows that Peter does 'not have in mind the things of God but the things of men'. The 'rock on which Jesus would build his church' has become 'a stumbling-block'.

But Jesus must also have heard in Peter's words an unmistakable echo of the voice that had kept whispering to him during his temptation in the desert. 'You don't need to go through all this suffering, you know. If you are the Son of God, there are other ways of fulfilling your saving mission. You could go instead for prestige, power and glory. This total self-sacrifice isn't strictly necessary . . .' This temptation was even more subtle and powerful than we sometimes realise. Jesus was being tempted not only to abandon the life of perfect *manhood* he had come to live, but to deny the very nature of his *Godhead* also. For, as Ian Bradley convincingly shows, self-sacrifice is the very essence of the life of the Trinitarian God himself.[2] Yes, Jesus had already had to face and overcome this temptation; now here it was again in the mouth of one of his best friends, one on whom he placed such great hopes for the future of his church. No wonder Jesus spun round and shouted 'Get behind me, Satan!'. Poor Peter; one moment he is uttering words of solicitous friendship, and the next Jesus seems to be hurling abuse at him. He must have wondered what had hit him! The fact is that Jesus' bolt was not

The Call to Sacrifice

directed at Peter himself, but at Satan, whom he recognised as speaking through Peter at that moment.

It is after this that Jesus spells out that all who would be his disciples must walk the same way and face the same cost as he himself. This makes the context (the Satanic origin of Peter's all-too-human response) significant for us also as we consider the contrast – the struggle, indeed – between self-centredness and self-sacrifice. With Satan's first entry into the drama of human history recorded in the Bible, precisely the same thing is happening. Just as Satan repeatedly came to Jesus with the question, 'Does it really have to be like this? If you really are the Son of God, surely it is within your power to change things, and do them your way?', so he came to our first parents with the insidious question 'Has God said . . . ?' They, too, were tempted not only to abandon their true humanity, but also to break the image of God (which, as we have briefly noted, includes self-sacrifice) in which they had been made. The Creator had given them everything they could need or desire, asking of them only obedience to his will. So the tempter really had only one point of attack at this stage: to suggest that they should reject God's will (of self-limitation) and assert their own (of self-gratification). He actually had the nerve to tell them that by being self-indulgent they would become 'like God'! From this point onward mankind gets two conflicting messages, one from the 'God of all truth' and the other from the 'father of lies':

> GOD: You are *already* made in my image, but if you stretch out your hand to the one thing

that is forbidden, that image will be broken and you will die.

SATAN: No; if you reach out and take it, you won't die; quite the opposite – it's then that you really *will* become like God.

GOD: By remaining within my will you can enjoy unbroken fellowship with me and experience the eternal life for which I created you.

SATAN: No; it is in following your own desires, in giving way to self-centredness, that you will find fulfilment and truly know what it is to live.

In whatever light we may choose to regard the Genesis account of creation, Eden and the Fall, it offers (for me at least) the only convincing explanation for the way things are – in particular for the plain fact that we are all instinctively self-centred. The battle for mankind's mind and will fought in Eden is the same battle that has been fought ever since, and still rages today. Because the battle against the original temptation was lost, so it is inherent in us to lose it time and again. This must be obvious to us all every day. Never mind the conflict between good and evil on the cosmic scale (which some find endlessly fascinating); in our own everyday experience it shows itself as our world-view *versus* God's; our will *versus* his; self-centredness *versus* self-sacrifice.

The 'Old' Nature and the 'New'

The New Testament defines 'a Christian' as someone who has recognised and repented of their

The Call to Sacrifice

sins and turned to Christ, receiving forgiveness through faith in his death on the cross.[3] And it teaches that the person who thus becomes a Christian receives a new nature from God, becoming a 'new creation' (2 Cor 5:17). At first sight it might be supposed then that, for the Christian, this battle of wills is all in the past, that the tendency to rebellion and self-centredness has been done away with. If only that were true! But experience tells us it is not. That is because the new nature which God gives us does not replace the old nature, but exists alongside it. This is an uncomfortable experience, because the two natures are as sharply different as they could possibly be, and lead in completely opposite directions. The old nature (the Bible calls it the lower or sinful nature, the natural man or the flesh) leads towards spiritual death: the new (higher or spiritual nature) leads to eternal life. The agony of these two natures co-existing in one person is poignantly described in Romans 7: Paul lays bare the problem, ending with the heartfelt cry: 'What a wretched man I am! Who will rescue me from this body of death?' (Rom 7:7–25). A permanent state of internal warfare between our old and new natures is the experience of Christians everywhere and in all ages. So it should come as no surprise that we still often find ourselves wanting to put our own happiness and fulfilment first. It is 'only natural': and that is precisely the problem. The fact is that such desires come from the 'natural man', the *old* nature; and, although as Christians we have to recognise that we still possess that old nature, we are called to live, not according to its demands, but in response to the promptings of the *new* nature God has given us:

> So I say, live by the Spirit, and you will not
> gratify the desires of the sinful nature. For
> the sinful nature desires what is contrary to
> the Spirit, and the Spirit what is contrary to
> the sinful nature.
>
> Those who belong to Christ Jesus have cru-
> cified the sinful nature with its passions and
> desires. Since we live by the Spirit, let us keep
> in step with the Spirit.
>
> (Gal 5:16–17; 24–25)

It is here that the going begins to get tough. Dietrich Bonhoeffer wrote: 'When Christ calls a man, he bids him come and die.[4] I wonder if that strikes you as a bit extreme. In fact it says no more than the Scriptures themselves say. The New Testament abounds with references to the Christian being 'crucified with Christ' (Gal 2:20), putting 'to death your earthly nature' (Col 3:5), and being so closely identified with Christ in his death as to 'count yourselves dead' to sin and self (Rom 6:1–14). Augustine (and later Luther) regarded being self-centred (*incurvatus in se*, or, literally, turned in on oneself) as the fundamental definition of sin, and salvation, therefore, as being delivered from that state. 'The greatest human malaise is self-preoccupation: the self in this state must be shattered and broken, or in Paul's words "crucified"'.[5]

The essence of Christ's death was that it represented total self-sacrifice for the supreme honour of God and the supreme good of others. Most of us can appreciate that idea without undue difficulty. But the cost of that self-sacrifice involved not only the horror of physical crucifixion, but also the rejection of his unconditional love by those he

The Call to Sacrifice

had come to save. Moreover, the Jewish religion saw the situation in which Jesus found himself as the ultimate proof of being under God's curse. That is what Paul means when he writes of Christ 'becoming a curse for us' (Gal 3:13), quoting from Deuteronomy 21:23 'anyone who is hung on a tree is under God's curse'. Modern people find it harder to appreciate fully these aspects of what Jesus' sacrifice cost him. Maybe that is why our awareness of the sacrificial element in the Christian faith has become dimmed. As Bonhoeffer writes:

> If our Christianity has ceased to be serious about discipleship, if we have watered down the gospel into emotional uplift which makes no costly demands . . . then we cannot help regarding the cross as an ordinary, everyday calamity, as one of the trials and tribulations of life. We have then forgotten that the cross means rejection and shame as well as suffering. The Psalmist was lamenting that he was despised and rejected of men, and that is an essential quality of the suffering of the cross. But this notion has ceased to be intelligible to a Christianity which can no longer see any difference between an ordinary human life and a life committed to Christ. The cross means sharing the suffering of Christ to the last and the fullest. Only a man thus totally committed to discipleship can experience the meaning of the cross.[6]

It is small wonder that Bonhoeffer, writing in Germany in 1937 as the shadow of the Second World War loomed, saw things in very stark terms. His acute awareness of the power of evil, and unswerving faithfulness in following the way of the Cross, eventually cost him his own life. For most of us – particularly the under-50s – the issues have not been so black and white. Of course some of us have suffered personal hardships – possibly even tragedies – but in general terms the society in which we have grown up and lived our lives has not presented us with such stark choices between obvious good and evil. In one way we have been fortunate in this: but in another I believe it has lulled us into a state of mind where we can easily forget the *cost* of discipleship as we enjoy (and rightly so) the assurance and security of it. This may well be the reason why we do not find it easy to appreciate the full significance of Christ's call to all those who would come after him to deny themselves, take up their cross and follow him.

Christ's death on the cross was not a last-minute rescue package put together by God. He is 'the Lamb that was slain from the creation of the world' (Rev 13:8). Yet, paradoxically, in that he was fully man as well as fully God, his sacrificial death was not 'inevitable' in the sense that he had no choice but to go through with it. We know that he was tempted to find an easier way, by those insidious voices in his head during the lonely fast in the desert, then again through Peter – and there must have been many other occasions. At the very last moment, in Gethsemane, shrinking from all that was involved, he desperately sought a way out. 'My Father,' he pleaded in agony, 'if it is possible, may this cup be taken from me.' At that moment, Jesus the man faced a real choice. He could have refused God's call to make the ultimate, shameful sacrifice – and was sorely tempted to do so. Instead, he uttered those final words on which our whole salvation depended: 'Yet not what I will, but what you will' (Mark 14:36). It was a conscious human act for Jesus to put the Father's will before his own. Remaining true to the nature of his Godhead, and fulfilling his own perfect manhood, he went to the cross to save mankind.

So, although we are not called to repeat his atoning death – which is unrepeatable – we must recognise the force of his call to us to follow him. It is a call to make a conscious act of will, just as he did. It means being ready to lead a life in which the honour of God and the good of others come before our own will; to accept that this will mean a constant and costly sacrifice of ourselves; to submit ourselves entirely as he did to the will of God, and in so doing to strive to abandon everything in ourselves which is self-pleasing.

The Pressures Against Sacrifice

So why do we find it so difficult – even distasteful – in the 1990s to take self-sacrifice on board as an essential part of what it means to be a Christian? As we have already observed, one reason is that the 'old' nature which is still in us constantly tells us that this is wrong and unnecessary; that God is being unreasonable in asking such obedience of us; that there must be a less costly way. This internal pressure (from the 'flesh and the devil') has been part of Christian experience from the beginning. But I believe there are additional pressures on us today (from 'the world') which bear down heavily on this aspect of discipleship.

The Welfare State – They Owe Me Something

First is the fact that, as I hinted above, many more people than in any previous generation have had life comparatively easy. Granted there have been in recent years major problems of unemployment and tough financial circumstances which have affected Christian and non-Christian families alike: I should not want to be insensitive to the hardships and sometimes traumas involved. But, whatever the shortcomings of the Welfare State, the fact remains that those of us brought up in the last fifty years have become so used to it that we do not really appreciate the circumstances in which our forbears lived, where there was simply nothing to fall back on when misfortune struck. I suppose it is inevitable that we have got used to the idea that life should be fairly comfortable; and, even more significantly, that the Government or somebody (usually referred to with delightful vagueness as 'they'!) owe it to us to see that it is. Most of us fail to realise that this way of thinking is comparatively new. The unquestioned assumption that things really *ought* to be all right for us, and that it is somebody's job to see that they are, is bound after a time to make it harder for us even to understand the concept of self-sacrifice, let alone to see it as the very basis of discipleship.

Political Correctness – The Ultimate Pressure to Conform

In the last decade or so, I believe it is the almost overwhelming influence of the media, advertising and other entirely secular forces which are shaping our society, and at the same time exerting non-stop pressures on us to 'conform' rather than

The Call to Sacrifice

to 'be transformed' (Rom 12:2). These pressures, once quite subtle, are becoming daily less so. The recent, and now inescapable, concept of 'political correctness' demonstrates the force of this. Being 'pc' is precisely about being 'conformed to the pattern of this world' – in many cases a pattern not even determined by the majority, but by the most strident or those with access to the means of exerting the most influence. They leave us in no doubt that disagreeing with them is not only patently stupid and wrongheaded, but potentially disadvantageous to ourselves – it shows that we are not worth listening to, not fit to hold responsibility, not to be taken seriously at all. The message of political correctness is blunt and brutal: conform or be damned.

Unfortunately, this does influence Christians, individually and collectively. Those (most of us) who live and work and play within the secular structures of the world are at particular risk here; they absorb its culture on a daily basis. A special challenge faces them – to learn to be 'in the world' but not 'of the world'; to recognise that the principles by which the world in general thinks and behaves are at best sub-Christian, and at worst anti-Christian. They have a special duty to be careful not to be the means of importing these worldly principles into the life of the Church. Unfortunately, there is ample evidence that the world's culture *has* entered into the Christian community in all kinds of ways – we shall be examining some of them in later chapters. On occasions this has happened consciously: more frequently, though, I believe Christians have simply not been aware of how they have transferred the world's ways of thinking into their personal, community and worshipping lives.

In this context, the significant thing which stands out most sharply is this. *In our society the idea of self-sacrifice is definitely, emphatically, NOT politically correct!* The correct emphasis today is on individuals maximising their opportunities for self-fulfilment and self-expression. In relating to one another, people's prime concern is to assert their rights over against the actions of others. These twin attitudes have increasingly shaped our view of individual relationships and society as a whole, to the point where they are, for most people, beyond questioning.

> I dare to assert that self-sacrifice rather than self-expression, a sense of duty rather than of rights, are the authentic marks of Christian discipleship.

If you are a Christian, a member of Christ's Body here on earth, and you think this assertion marks me down either as a reactionary who has not kept up with modern thinking, or as a bit of a fanatic with a bee in his bonnet – you may, of course, be right! Or it may be that you are living proof of my assertion that the pattern of this world's thinking has so far infiltrated Christian minds that it appears to many in sharper focus than does the call of Christ. Paul sets out very clearly the attitude which is truly Christ-like:

> Do nothing out of selfish ambition or vain conceit, but in humility consider others better than yourselves. Each of you should look not only to your own interests, but also to the interests of others.

> Your attitude should be the same as that of Christ Jesus:
> Who, being in very nature God,
> did not consider equality with God something to be grasped,
> but made himself nothing,
> taking the very nature of a servant, being made in human likeness.
> And being found in appearance as a man,
> he humbled himself
> and became obedient to death – even death on a cross!
>
> (Phil 2:3–8)

Health, Wealth and Happiness – The Christian's Right?

We might expect that when the Christian, assaulted by the world's values for most of the time, meets with fellow-believers for worship, prayer and teaching, he or she will receive a strong dose of corrective teaching about the way of the Cross. Sadly, this is often not the case. Many churches today seem to fail their members here, not only by sins of omission (failing to issue the challenge of Christ's call to self-sacrifice), but also sins of commission (actively teaching and encouraging the very self-centredness which Christ calls them to deny). I am aware that this is a very serious charge. I do not make it (in the words of the Book of Common Prayer) 'unadvisedly or lightly' but 'soberly and in the fear of God'. It is born of over thirty years of hearing sermons and attending services and meetings of various kinds. It reflects a distinct and observable shift of emphasis in much Christian teaching over the last ten to fifteen years towards what might loosely be called the 'pleasure principle'.

It is no part of genuine Christian faith to avoid or disapprove of all kinds of legitimate pleasure: God 'richly provides us with everything for our enjoyment' (1 Tim 6:17). But our society today is *obsessed* with the pursuit of pleasure. If you doubt this, just look more critically than usual at a random selection of TV ads. The materialism of the 1960s and 70s, which concentrated mainly on the acquisition of *things*, has been replaced in the 1990s by the lure of enjoyable *experiences*. The really desirable prizes on TV game shows are the holidays. The Reader's Digest tells us that the pleasure of winning that luxury car (which you cannot afford to run!) is how you – and the neighbours – will *feel* when you see it standing on your drive. There seems to be no limit to the number of theme parks the world can support, each promising more lavish (and more terrifying!) experiences than the others. The weekend papers are full of suggestions for presents to the one you love – trips in a hot air balloon or driving a Formula One car round a racing circuit. Great! But whereas the dangers for the Christian of the more objective 'thing-based' materialism were obvious, this more subjective 'experience-based' version is far less easily recognised for the potential trap that it is. Yet for our lives to be shaped by the pursuit, or even the expectation, of pleasing experiences is both wrong and spiritually dangerous.

It is especially dangerous at this time because it has coincided with an emphasis on 'experience-centred' religion in many parts of the Church. This may, of course, be no coincidence. If my general thesis is correct, it may be a direct result of the Church uncritically absorbing this aspect of worldly culture. Whether this be so or not, it ought to be a matter of desperate concern that, just at the point

The Call to Sacrifice

where the Church ought to be issuing a forceful challenge to the world's pleasure-seeking principle, it is often to be found not only accommodating, but actually re-inforcing it. 'You deserve to look this good,' says the hair-conditioner advert. 'You deserve to be happy and in good health,' says the preacher. Whether it is the full-blown 'prosperity gospel' found in the United States and elsewhere, or the apparently less extravagant offer of healing from every illness or discomfort, the basic notion is that you are entitled to expect a pleasant life because you are God's child. J I Packer has said:

> Feelings of pleasure and comfort, springing from pleasant circumstances and soothing experiences, are prime goals these days, and much Christianity on both sides of the Atlantic tries to oblige us by manufacturing them for us. Sometimes, as a means to this end, it invokes the idea that God's promises are like a magician's spells: use them correctly and you can extract from God any legitimate pleasant thing you wish.[7]

This type of teaching (aptly summarised as 'name it, claim it and frame it'!) starts from the premise that happiness consists in the experience of pleasure and freedom from everything we find unpleasant. Having made that first cardinal error, it is but a short step to assert that 'we may confidently look to God here and now to shield us from unpleasantness at every turn, or, if unpleasantness breaks in, to deliver us from it immediately . . .'[8] This slippery slope is equally lethal whether the succession of pleasant experiences we believe we should expect from God are of a material or a spiritual nature.

'Cardinal error' is a strong phrase! I refer to the idea that, in willing our greatest good (or 'happiness'), God promises us roses all the way. In the light of the consistent revelation of Scripture, that is profoundly wrong. We shall examine this fully in the next chapter. Meanwhile, it ought to be self-evident that the call to sacrifice will frequently mean laying down our own comfort, well-being, desires and inclinations, for the good of others, the sake of the gospel or our own longer-term spiritual health and development. And, to return to where we began, we cannot dismiss this or regard it as an optional part of Christian experience. As Bonhoeffer points out, Peter's unthinking attempt to divert Jesus himself from the path to the cross shows how the idea of a suffering Messiah was an affront even to the first disciples; we can see, in embryo, the future Church of Christ already resisting the law of suffering being enjoined on it by its Lord. He goes on:

> Jesus must therefore make it clear beyond all doubt that the 'must' of suffering applies to his disciples no less than to himself. Just as Christ is Christ only in virtue of his suffering and rejection, so the disciple is a disciple only in so far as he shares his Lord's suffering and rejection and crucifixion. Discipleship means adherence to the person of Jesus, and therefore submission to the law of Christ which is the law of the cross.[9]

TWO
THE CONTEXT OF SACRIFICE

Do not store up for yourselves treasures on earth . . . But store up for yourselves treasures in heaven . . . For where your treasure is, there your heart will be also.

(Matt 6:19–21)

Dear friends, now we are children of God, and what we will be has not yet been made known. But we know that when he appears, we shall be like him, for we shall see him as he is.

(1 John 3:2)

Changed from glory into glory,
Till in heaven we take our place;
Till we cast our crowns before Thee,
Lost in wonder, love and praise.

(Charles Wesley)[1]

Try to imagine living in Jesus' time, even being one of his closest friends. One day Jesus says, 'I know this is amazing, but after I have died I am going to do something no one has ever done before – three days later I shall rise from the dead.' You reply, 'No! This shall never happen to you' Can you believe it? Of course not; that would be a ridiculous response. There would have to be something very wrong with you if you did not want this wonderful thing to happen to your best friend. Yet, as we have just seen, that was exactly how Peter reacted. Why? Because that was not all Jesus said about his future. First, he said, he must suffer many things and be killed – and after that be raised to life again. Peter was so horrified by the first part of Jesus' news that he never even listened to what followed.

A good friend of mine who is a retired surgeon says that many years of dealing with patients has taught him that people always tend to react like this. They came to him for the results of medical investigations; and, if the first minute contained something they feared, they simply did not hear the rest of what he had to say, even though it may have been reassuring. That is just how it was with Peter. As soon as he heard 'suffer' and 'die', Peter's mind went into overdrive. How could it be that this suffering was going to be inflicted on his friend by the religious authorities? And what unspeakable things were going to happen to Jesus? And, in view of Peter's subsequent behaviour at Jesus' arrest and trial, I do not think we do him an injustice by suggesting that it may already have registered, 'If Jesus suffers and dies, what happens to me? They all know I've been with him . . .'. While all this was racing through Peter's mind, Jesus had been saying 'and on the third day I shall be raised to life'. Peter was there when the announcement was made of the greatest event in human history, and he actually missed it! We must not be too hard on him, though, because it seems that all the other disciples also failed to pick it up. What is more,

The Context of Sacrifice

all three Synoptic Gospels show that Jesus had already tried to teach them about his forthcoming death and resurrection. John shows how he also tried to put it across less directly to his disciples – for example where he talks about their grief turning to joy (John 16:16–22) – and to a wider audience when he spoke about the authorities destroying 'this temple' and his raising it again in three days (John 2:19–22). That passage ends by saying that it was not until after Jesus was risen that 'his disciples recalled what he had said' and began to believe both 'the Scripture and the words that Jesus had spoken' (John 2:22).

Even this hindsight was somewhat slow to operate. In fact, Luke 24 depicts three groups of believers being ticked off for failing either to remember what he had said or to understand and believe their Scriptures:

- The women who came to the tomb needed two angels to jog their memories: 'Why look for Jesus here? Don't you remember what he told you . . . ?' They rushed back to tell the other disciples, who still did not believe them; the women's words 'seemed to them like nonsense'. Peter rushed off to see the empty tomb for himself, but left the scene 'wondering to himself what had happened' – still the penny did not drop (Luke 24:1–12). (John, it seems, believed but did not understand – see John 20:3–9.)

- The two disciples on the Emmaus road heard their unknown companion accuse them of being 'foolish and slow to believe the prophets'; and still they did not recognise him until he made himself known in breaking bread (Luke 24:13–35).

- The whole band of disciples were gently upbraided when Christ appeared in the upper room: 'Why do doubts rise in your minds? . . . This is what I told you . . . Everything must be fulfilled that is written about me in the Law of Moses, the Prophets and the Psalms' (Luke 24:36–49).

I have dwelt on this because I believe it is so typical of the way we ourselves are inclined to think and behave. To be blunt about it, we often cannot see beyond the end of our own spiritual noses! We have abundant evidence that our life in this world is only a part of something far greater and altogether more magnificent. Compared to those first disciples we have it all laid out on a plate. Yet we either 'stubbornly refuse to believe' like the bulk of the disciples, or we 'wonder what is happening', or (at best) like John we 'believe but still do not understand'. Is it not true that for most of the time we carry on in the routine of daily life and in our church worship and fellowship as if this world is all there is?

One of the Iona Community's lovely liturgies asks God that we may have 'the perspective of your kingdom in which to see the things of earth'.[2] Amen! That hits the nail squarely on the head. That would put many aspects of our Christian lives into the right perspective: but in the context of self-sacrifice it is no exaggeration to say that without such a perspective we shall never be able to come to terms with Christ's call to deny ourselves, take up our cross daily, and follow him.

Death and Resurrection

Paul wrote: 'And [Jesus] died for all, that those who live should no longer live for themselves but for him who died for them and was raised again' (2 Cor 5:15). Here, in relation to sacrificial living (living not 'for ourselves' but 'for Jesus'), Paul establishes the inseparable connection between Christ's death and his resurrection. It is crucial to understand this. However much we may (and must) rely on Christ's death on the cross as the place where he bore our sins and the sins of the whole world, it remains true that the cross is incomplete without the resurrection. At his baptism, and again at his transfiguration, God had declared 'You are my Son, whom I love; with you I am well pleased'. It had been in his complete obedience to his Father's will, whatever the cost to himself, that Jesus had most clearly demonstrated his true sonship. By raising him from the dead the Father declares again, emphatically and unequivocally, the Sonship of Christ (Rom 1:4) and his own acceptance of the Son's sacrificial obedience. Henceforth, accepting 'death' becomes the way to 'life'. Christ was not raised *in spite of* dying the most shameful death possible ('anyone who is hung on a tree is under God's curse') but precisely *because* of it: 'And being found in appearance as a man, he humbled himself and became obedient to death – even death on a cross! *Therefore* God exalted him to the highest place and gave him the name that is above every name . . .' (Phil 2:8–9 my italics).

It is vital to understand this. The 'therefore' means the link between Christ's sacrificial death and his mighty resurrection life is not accidental, but inevitable. As the old song used to say (but about something quite different!) 'you can't have one without the other'. In forging this unbreakable link Christ sets the pattern for all those who would follow him. He promises that 'Because I live, you also will live' (John 14:19). That same pattern is spelt out elsewhere in the New Testament:

> Here is a trustworthy saying:
> If we died with him,
> we will also live with him;
> if we endure, we will also reign with him.
> (2 Tim 2:11–12)

> Or don't you know that all of us who were baptised into Christ Jesus were baptised into his death? We were therefore buried with him through baptism into death in order that, just as Christ was raised from the dead through the glory of the Father, we too may live a new life.
> If we have been united with him like this in his death, we will certainly also be united with him in his resurrection . . .
> Now if we died with Christ, we believe that we will also live with him.
> (Rom 6:3–5, 8)

Repeatedly the call for Christians to be identified with Christ in his death is linked with the promise of sharing in his resurrection. 'You may be suffering now,' Peter wrote later, 'but you still rejoice in your "living hope through the resurrection of Jesus Christ"' (1 Pet 1:3–7). This is the ultimate 'feel-good' factor! But, of course, the proposition is equally true in reverse: if we are to share in his resurrection, we must first share in his

The Context of Sacrifice

sufferings. Sometimes Paul actually stated it that way round: 'I want to know Christ and the power of his resurrection and the fellowship of sharing in his sufferings, becoming like him in his death, and so, somehow, to attain to the resurrection of the dead' (Phil 3:10–11).

Now although we have noted that there is an inevitability about the way death leads to resurrection, suffering to glory, sacrifice to reward, Paul (even with his education and spiritual wisdom) did not claim to understand it. It remained a mystery. He says 'and so, *somehow*, to attain to the resurrection . . .' It is one of those aspects of Christian truth (actually this applies to most of them!) which can only be perceived by faith – the kind of faith Charles Wesley demonstrated when he wrote in his great Easter hymn:

> Soar we now where Christ has led,
> Following our exalted Head;
> Made like him, like him we rise;
> Ours the cross, the grave, the skies.
> Alleluia![3]

Failure to perceive and believe this causes us to flinch and draw back from the call to sacrifice, making it appear 'a negative doctrine of self-destruction and humiliation' rather than the promise of 'the transfiguring glory of resurrection' which it actually is.[4]

The Divine Order

Yet, to live Christianly, we *must* perceive and believe it, because what we have here is nothing less than a divine order which runs through the whole universe. Filling and shaping everything, it is as inescapable as it is universal. It runs like this:

First comes the suffering – then the glory.

First the cross – then the crown.

First the sacrifice – then the reward.

Now we may not like this too much at first sight. This is because the 'old nature' still at work in us instinctively rebels against it: 'For the sinful nature desires what is contrary to the Spirit, and the Spirit what is contrary to the sinful nature. They are in conflict with each other, so that you do not do what you want' (Gal 5:17).

But for late 20th-century Christians it is also partly due, once again, to our conditioning. The fact is that this divine order is the opposite of what we have become used to in our daily lives. The motto in Western society today is 'have it now, pay later'. That is the basis of things many of us have taken for granted for years, such as mortgages on our homes. And it is the principle on which a great deal of consumerism is based. Get your new central heating system or double-glazing now, before the winter starts – nothing to pay until next March. This makes a good deal of sense from everybody's point of view. You get your warmth in time for the cold weather, the company secures your business now ('a bird in the hand . . .' and all that!), and later on they get more of your money as a result of the interest you will pay for the privilege of deferred payments.

The Context of Sacrifice

There is nothing intrinsically wrong in this as a way of doing business (though there are dangers to the imprudent). But if we unconsciously allow ourselves to think that spiritual things work, or ought to work, in the same way, then we are in real trouble. The cosmic order of things runs the opposite way.

> In the divine scheme, the one who loses his life gains it; the one who humbles himself is lifted up; strength comes through weakness; the first shall be last and the last first. Above all, it is in dying that we live.

This inescapable fact of spiritual life reflects the relationship between Jesus' sacrifice and its reward (in his case the ultimates of death and resurrection):

> We must live sacrificially in order to experience the reward.
>
> We must be prepared to 'share his sufferings' in order to 'reign with him'.
>
> We must be ready for 'the cross' in order to be certain of receiving 'the crown'.

The Church of England's Collect for the third Sunday in Lent is a prayer we might well use throughout the year:

> Almighty God, whose most dear Son went not up to joy but first he suffered pain, and entered not into glory before he was crucified: mercifully grant that we, walking in the way

of the cross, may find it none other than the way of life and peace; through Jesus Christ our Lord.

The Earthbound Perspective

I should not be surprised if this all strikes many readers as rather hard, or even unfair. If so, then that only serves to demonstrate how far the world's way of thinking has invaded the Christian community. It has done so to such an extent that it has had serious consequences for the way multitudes of Christians hold their faith. We have become what I called earlier 'earthbound'. This does not just mean that we are unwilling to let go of material possessions. In some Christian quarters today there is such an emphasis on health and wellbeing as to suggest that it is the Number One thing on God's agenda for us – and sometimes, sadly, those who hold this view are less than charitable towards those who think differently. It might sound contradictory, but it is even possible to be 'earthbound' in relation to the life of the Spirit. It has been well said that in many modern worship songs the 'grand theme is Ourselves'. We can be totally taken up with our acquisition, use and enjoyment of spiritual gifts. Yet Paul asserts that they are just temporary; one day we shall experience a state of direct 'face-to-faceness' which we cannot yet grasp or define, when prophecies, tongues and words of knowledge will all cease. If we think that's bad news, we're spiritually earthbound!

This is no new phenomenon. While Jesus was still on earth, there were many who followed him

The Context of Sacrifice

because of the miracles he performed. In John 6 it is clear that many went after him for what they could get (signs and wonders, v 2; political leadership, v 15; food, v 26). When Jesus went on to speak of himself as the bread of life which, if anyone eats, he will live for ever, they said 'This is a hard teaching. Who can accept it?' (v 60). It was when he finally spelt out that he was offering not material things, but spiritual communion with himself, that 'many of his disciples turned back and no longer followed him' (John 6:1–66). With great sadness Jesus asked the Twelve, 'You do not want to leave too, do you?'. This time Peter did have the long-term vision, replying, 'Lord, to whom shall we go? You have the words of eternal life.' Sadly, in our own time it is still at that point that many who have been following Jesus for more tangible blessings turn back.

There is no question but that we are similarly earthbound today. It is an observable fact that what fills our thoughts and guides our actions are maximum well-being and fulfilment here and now. If heaven comes into it at all, it is as an after-thought. I am not alone in believing that this limited perspective has become a major disease affecting the Church in our time. Dr Jim Packer addresses this in some detail in his book *Laid-Back Religion*. He writes that, among the secular pressures which have proved too much for the rather loosely-held 'pietistic asceticism' inherited largely (he believes) from 18th- and 19th-century evangelicalism in Britain and America, 'humanism has touted individual self-expression, self-discovery, self-realization, and self-fulfilment as life's supreme goal. Christians have taken this thought into their minds and affirmed that this is God's will too.'[5]

The reason for this, he believes, is that for the most part Christians today 'no longer live for heaven'. We have 'recast Christianity into a mould that stresses happiness above holiness, blessings here above blessedness hereafter, health and wealth as God's best gifts, and death . . . as the supreme disaster'.

He concludes that our Christianity is now 'out of shape', the basic reason being that

> we have lost the New Testament's two-world perspective that views the next life as more important than this one and understands life here as essentially preparation and training for the life hereafter. And we shall continue out of shape till this proper other-worldliness is recovered. Such other-worldliness does not in any way imply a low view of the wonder and glory and richness that life in this world can have. What other-worldliness implies is that you live your life here . . . making your decisions in terms of your knowledge of being a traveller on the way home.[6]

He is absolutely right, of course. If we can only escape from our 'this-worldly' conditioning as we read the New Testament, we shall be able to discern an insistent 'upward call'. Let me remind you of one or two of the most direct examples.

There is the command of Christ himself:

> 'Do not store up for yourselves treasures on earth, where moth and rust destroy, and where thieves break in and steal. But store up for yourselves treasures in heaven, where moth and rust do not destroy, and where

> thieves do not break in and steal. For where your treasure is, there your heart will be also.
>
> (Matt 6:19–21)

There is Paul:

> Since, then, you have been raised with Christ, set your hearts on things above, where Christ is seated at the right hand of God. Set your minds on things above, not on earthly things. For you died, and your life is now hidden with Christ in God.
>
> (Col 3:1–3)

Elsewhere he emphasises the contrast between unbelievers (he calls them sharply 'enemies of the cross of Christ') whose 'mind is on earthly things' and Christian believers whose 'citizenship is in heaven' (Phil 3:19–20). This same concept is echoed by the writer of the letter to the Hebrews: 'For here we do not have an enduring city, but we are looking for the city that is to come' (Heb 13:14).

Looking Onwards and Upwards

This then is the context in which God's word envisages his children living out the whole of their lives. Aware that they are moving on, they set their eyes on their true home in heaven, not getting too tied down by the things of this world. 'Cling lightly to that which is not eternal,' said John Wesley. If we have not learnt to live consciously in the death-resurrection, suffering-glory, sacrifice-reward divine order, this may well seem a 'hard saying'. If we have so learnt, this sense of detachment from the world – both its joys and its sorrows – will be becoming part of our experience of daily life as God's children. At our Christian best, we shall 'show by every word and gesture that [we] do not belong to this earth' (Bonhoeffer)[7]; at least it will be (as it was for Paul) the goal towards which we aim. Indeed, the acceptance into our very selves of this divine order is one of the marks by which we may be assured of our standing as his children:

> The Spirit himself testifies with our spirit that we are God's children. Now if we are children, then we are heirs – heirs of God and co-heirs with Christ, if indeed we share in his sufferings in order that we may also share in his glory.
>
> (Rom 8:16–17)

Now I think I can almost hear you protesting: 'But we just don't think like that nowadays. People can't go round dreaming about heaven all the time: that's the way to become so heavenly-minded that we're no earthly use. Are you really saying the Christian life is a matter of gritting our teeth and putting up with all sorts of deprivation here in the expectation of receiving "pie in the sky when we die"?' No, nothing of the sort. It is all much more positive than that. As Bonhoeffer says: '. . . the cross is not the terrible end to an otherwise God-fearing and happy life, but . . . the beginning of our communion with Christ.'[8]

Ian Bradley similarly emphasises that this giving up of self is not somehow to step out of

The Context of Sacrifice

'real life' – rather to opt into life as God means it to be. Not something for 'saints and spiritual super-heroes',

> ... it is a gift that God in his mercy and wisdom has made available to us all. We fulfil his purposes, and also conform ourselves with the rest of his creation, by playing our part in the great Divine economy of sacrifice, however uncertainly or imperfectly. To live sacrificially is to beat time with the rhythm of life.[9]

Learning to look through the 'here-and-now' to the 'beyond' is a good starting point in seeking to 'follow' Jesus by making him the example for our discipleship. Did you know that, in his own experience of being human, it was Jesus' ability to look *through* the suffering to the glory beyond it that kept him going? It was this which gave him the inner strength not to turn aside from the horror and shame, but to go obediently to the Cross. This is what the writer to the Hebrews asserts, exhorting us to face life with the same attitude:

> ... let us run with perseverance the race marked out for us. Let us fix our eyes on Jesus, the author and perfecter of our faith, who *for the joy set before him* endured the cross, scorning its shame, and sat down at the right hand of the throne of God. Consider him who endured such opposition from sinful men, so that you will not grow weary and lose heart.
>
> (Heb 12:1–3; italics mine)

'Let us fix our eyes on Jesus . . .'; and, as the old chorus says, 'the things of earth will grow strangely dim in the light of his glory and grace'. There lies the secret. The New Testament reveals a truth about our human lives which is amazing in its implications. It is not just that we should try to follow him, but that once our eyes are single-mindedly fixed on him (i.e., we are totally committed to following him) then everything that happens to us is a part of a process of being made more like him. How often the comforting words of Romans 8:28 about 'all things working together for our good' are quoted – sometimes more in desperation than confident faith – when the going gets tough. If they were taken in their context, they would be at once more demanding and more comforting:

> And we know that in all things God works for the good of those who love him, who have been called according to his purpose. For those God foreknew he also predestined to be conformed to the likeness of his Son, that he might be the firstborn among many brothers. And those he predestined, he also called; those he called, he also justified; those he justified, he also glorified.
>
> (Rom 8:28–30)

Being 'conformed to the likeness' of God's Son means being shaped according to the image or pattern of Jesus. We have already seen what that pattern is – the acceptance of the path through suffering to glory. Everything that comes our way, 'good' or 'bad' as we may think it, is a part of this process.

The Context of Sacrifice

* * *

But the full revelation of what it means to be Christian is even more positive than that.

> It is not just that everything that happens to us is designed to make us more like Jesus: the fact is that this growing Christ-likeness is the very purpose for which we were created.

'Dear friends, now we are children of God, and what we will be has not yet been made known. But we know that when he appears, we shall be like him, for we shall see him as he is' (1 John 3:2).

This verse ought to be on the desk in every preacher and pastor's study, and over the bathroom mirror and kitchen sink of every Christian home! It puts into the proper perspective everything that happens to us each day. It reminds us that we are on the way to a fulfilment so amazing that it blows the mind. As Dr Martyn Lloyd-Jones says, 'If we but grasped this, it would revolutionise our lives ... everything else pales into insignificance'.[10] Indeed, revolutionising our lives is just what John says it should do, for he goes on in the following verse to say that 'everyone who has this hope in him purifies himself' (1 John 3:3). A key idea in the concept of 'purity' here (as in the Beatitude about the 'pure in heart', where the promise is also the same — that they will see God) is single-mindedness, the determination to keep oneself free from distracting influences.

Another way of saying the same thing would be to speak of becoming 'holy'. The concept of holiness is, in fact, intertwined with that of sacrifice. The very word 'sacrifice' comes from root words in

Latin which mean to 'make holy'. Realising this adds a new dimension to our understanding.

> The word sacrifice in our language means always losing something ... But ... in all the ancient languages, sacrifice comes from sacred – it means to make something ... holy and not to lose it. Indeed when you bring a life to God or a gift to God, it becomes His, it is no longer yours in the greedy and possessive sense of the word. But it becomes holy with the holiness of God.[11]

The promise of ultimately being *completely* like Christ is, then, not only the distant prospect. Growing Christ-likeness – or, put another way, growing acceptance of self-sacrifice – is also the thing that we are to pursue single-mindedly throughout our lives, the goal from which we must not let ourselves be distracted by other influences. This is growth in holiness. It is to be the guiding principle which shapes our attitudes and behaviour now: 'just as he who called you is holy, so be holy in all you do' (1 Pet 1:15). The process of Christian living can be summed up as 'being transformed into his likeness with ever-increasing glory' (2 Cor 3:18). Both the ultimate promise, and the present process which leads towards its fulfilment, together form the backdrop against which the call to sacrificial living, or holiness, must be viewed.

Living and Dying

Before leaving these foundation-laying chapters it is worth adding that, once we are able to outgrow our earthbound mind-set, this can revolutionise our approach not only to living as Christians, but also to dying as Christians. Dietrich Bonhoeffer's last reported words, shortly before the death squad came for him, were: 'This is the end – for me it is the beginning of life.' This clearly reflects his own deeply sacrificial discipleship. But surely it is also evidence of an ability to see this life and the next as a single piece: it was this which enabled him to live so single-mindedly and die so courageously. But this is not just for heroes. Such a perspective will enable us all to see death not only as an end, but as a new beginning. Then the idea of death as the ultimate healing of all that keeps us from full communion with God becomes not just a nice (or even daring) abstract idea, but the very touchstone of the way we live our Christian lives and prepare for a Christian death. It is possible then to see the main purpose of living this life as enabling us to die this death. It makes accepting self-denial, rather than self-fulfilment, not a life-denying, but a life-affirming, philosophy. Charles Wesley knew this when he wrote his great hymn 'O Thou who camest from above' about sacrificial living, a life in which our heart's desire is to 'work and speak and think' for Jesus:

> Ready for all Thy perfect will,
> My acts of faith and love repeat;
> Till death Thy endless mercies seal,
> And make the sacrifice complete.[12]

In our own time, the contemplative nun Maria Boulding, reflecting on life lived in sacrificial surrender to the will of God, writes that 'death will be the best part of living, the thing for which you have been practising'.[13]

Similarly, Paul's desire 'to depart and be with Christ, which is better by far' (Phil 1:23) was not just the classic Freudian 'death-wish' – which would have been understandable since he was at the time languishing in chains in a Roman prison. It was a positive expression of his unshakable conviction of the continuity of our experience of Christ here and hereafter. 'For to me, to live is Christ and to die is gain' (Phil 1:21). Here he was suffering with Christ; hereafter he would reign with him. Because he had this long perspective he was able to see, from the very depths of what his sacrifice for the gospel's sake cost him, to the glory that lay beyond. So Paul was able to embrace death, not as putting an end to what his life had been about, but as its fulfilment.

* * *

Before we go on to look in practical detail at some of the ways in which the principle of self-sacrifice might be worked out in our daily lives, it will be as well to sum up what we have considered in this chapter:

- Christians are promised a share in the glory of Christ's resurrection, but in order to receive the promise they must first be ready to follow him along the self-sacrificial way of the Cross.

- This represents a divine order (suffering-glory, cross-crown, sacrifice-reward, death-resurrection), which we cannot alter.

The Context of Sacrifice

- We must learn that the promised future of resurrection life with Christ is just as real and certain as the present life of following him in self-denial.

- It is necessary – though maybe not 'politically-correct' even in Christian circles – to see this life as only part of the process of God's work in us, a process to be completed after death. This is not escapism, but the only true perspective in which to see the call to live sacrificially here and now.

- The whole purpose of this life is to develop the life of God in us so that we become 'conformed to the image of his Son'. This growing Christ-likeness now will lead to the ultimate completion of God's purpose for his children, to be like Christ 'when he appears'. That will be our individual part in the glorious consummation of all things in him through whom, and for whom, all things were made.

In the light of all this, the call to live sacrificially is not God placing some kind of hard or unfair imposition on us. Rather it is him inviting us, his unworthy children, to share in the very nature of the Godhead by becoming 'conformed to the image of his Son'.

> Self-sacrifice is the first step on a pathway of unspeakable privilege which leads to a destiny of unimaginable glory.

If we are filled with the love of Christ, the power of his Holy Spirit and the vision to discern what lies ahead, we shall find that 'his commands are not burdensome' (1 John 5:3). Sacrifice is, indeed, 'profoundly liberating'.[14] The Christ who calls us to deny ourselves, take up our cross and follow him also said 'my yoke is easy and my burden is light' (Matt 11:30). We can be sure of this – and we should do well to recall it whenever we feel sorry for ourselves along the sacrificial road – whatever God may ask of us, it will not amount to a millionth part of what Jesus himself bore for us. Isaac Watts knew this when he wrote,

> Were the whole realm of nature mine,
> That were an offering far too small;
> Love so amazing, so divine,
> Demands my life, my soul, my all![15]

THREE
CHURCH LIFE – (1) THE SACRIFICIAL PATTERN

This is how we know what love is: Jesus Christ laid down his life for us. And we ought to lay down our lives for our brothers.

(1 John 3:16)

The biblical concept of laying down our lives for others seems far removed from so much of what we now call 'church'. Perhaps we have emphasised the fun, fulfilment and fellowship aspects of Christianity to the detriment of the concept of sacrificial love.

(Steve Chalke)[1]

The New Testament uses several metaphors to describe the Church, including a building, an army and a bride. But the most frequent and well-developed metaphor is the 'body' – specifically the Body of Christ. It forms the basis of teaching about the mutual life of the Church's members (e.g. 1 Cor 12:12–26; Col 3:15); its use of spiritual gifts (Rom 12:4–8); its essential unity (Eph 4:1–12); the equality of Jew and Gentile within the Church (Eph 2:14–18; 3:6); its sacramental life (1 Cor 10:16–17); its relationship with Christ, its Head (Col 1:18, 24; Eph 4:15), and its ultimate glorious destiny (Eph 1:22–23).

One can imagine other equally personal metaphors which might fittingly have been used to identify the Church closely with its Lord and Founder – the 'Personality of Christ' to describe the entity left behind after he had departed, or the 'Philosophy of Christ' for those committed to his teaching. But no: the Church is called the 'Body of Christ', despite the fact that his *body* was precisely the part of him which was no longer around. Or, maybe, not despite that fact, but because of it. Consider that:

- it was in his *human* body that he had fully identified with the fallen race he came to save;
- it was in his *broken* body on the cross that he offered the sacrifice that atoned for sin, and opened the way to forgiveness and a restored relationship between mankind and God;
- it was in his *resurrection* body that he broke the bands of death and demonstrated the reality of the new life which awaits all who follow him.

In short, it is in his *body* – a human body both before and after his resurrection – that the principle of sacrifice is both demonstrated and vindicated. This is immensely significant. It means that the Church, the Body of Christ, the successor to his earthly body, is to

- identify with a world in need of salvation;
- express its life in a sacrificial way; and

- proclaim in both word and deed that new quality of life which is at once the result of his resurrection and the foreshadowing of ours.

In fact, this is a fair summary of the very reason for the Church's existence. The Church is the redeemed community, brought into being and sustained by Christ's sacrificial death and triumphant resurrection. It is surely here, then, that we should find the sacrificial principle and the expectation of glory recognised, valued, taught and put into practice.

> Called to be 'transformed' in this world, not 'conformed' to it, it is only as it lives out this 'sacrifice-glory' principle that the Church is seen to be the Body of Christ. This ought to make it distinctively, even startlingly, different from the world.

In considering the far-reaching practical implications of this, there is a danger of which we must be aware. All of us find it only too easy to talk about 'the Church' as some abstract entity. So we shall constantly need to remind ourselves that the Church is made up of its individual members. (I am not forgetting the 'communion of saints': but in this book we must concentrate on that part of the Church presently on earth.) So when we are thinking about the local church, it is not about 'them' – the minister and Parochial Church Council, the Elders or church committee – but about 'us' – you and me. What *we* are, and how *we* think and behave, determines what our church is like. Similarly we must see the wider church not as some remote hierarchical structure. Try to think of your own church in its local community as part of the universal Church in the world.

Three Principles from the Example of Christ

We have already considered how Christ's own sacrifice, and his call to follow him in self-denial, leave no choice but to equate discipleship with self-sacrifice. Now from that broad picture we zoom in closer on the Gospels' account of his life, and the teaching of the earliest Christian leaders. In particular we see how our Lord himself interacted with other people. As this comes into sharper focus, we can observe three principles which I suggest ought to be the model for all our thinking about being his Body on earth today.

(1)   He put others before himself.

(2)   He paid special attention to the needs of the poor, the weak, and those on the margins of society.

(3)   He looked for, and brought about, major change in the lives of those he met.

Putting Others First
Jesus seems always to have been ministering to others. Remember he was human. He got tired just as you and I do, and no doubt (just like us) he sometimes found people a bit of a pain! But he seems always to have made himself available. He even got diverted to heal one person while on his way to heal another (Matt 9:18–26). Although he

Church Life – (1) The Sacrificial Pattern

guarded his times alone with his Father, we never read of him turning away someone in need. In the end he paid the supreme cost of this complete selflessness. Putting *everybody* else before himself, he died for the sins of the whole world, though we were all unworthy of his love. His approach is an example for us all. The Bible leaves us in no doubt about that: 'This is how we know what love is: Jesus Christ laid down his life for us. And we ought to lay down our lives for our brothers' (1 John 3:16).

Christians recognise that it is through that sacrificial death that we have received forgiveness of our sins and a new life of 'eternal' quality. Since our very life thus depends on Christ's own selflessness, we, above all other people, should appreciate that following him will mean us being unselfish too. It is a truism (but none the less true!) that the shape of the cross represents a capital 'I' crossed out. Amongst those who share this awareness, therefore, it is not unreasonable to expect to find this principle of 'others first' shaping our relationships and underlying all our actions. Looking at the New Testament we do indeed find this presented as the normative pattern of Christian fellowship. Paul put it succinctly to the Roman Christians: 'Be devoted to one another in brotherly love. Honour one another above yourselves' (Rom 12:10).

And again to the Corinthians: 'Nobody should seek his own good, but the good of others' (1 Cor 10:24).

To the Philippians he spelt it out rather more fully:

> . . . make my joy complete by being likeminded, having the same love, being one in

spirit and purpose. Do nothing out of selfish
ambition or vain conceit, but in humility
consider others better than yourselves. Each
of you should look not only to your own
interests, but also to the interests of others.
(Phil 2:2–4)

This should be Christians' attitude towards one another (he went on) because it is 'the same as that of Christ Jesus' who, despite being Lord of all ('in very nature God') was prepared to become human and accept a death of pain and disgrace for the sake of others (Phil 2:5–8). We cannot ask for a clearer example than that. We cannot pretend we do not know what putting others first means. We are called to follow our Lord. It is in the church that we are surrounded by others with this common understanding and purpose. Surely, then, this should be the place where our willingness to 'deny ourselves' can be seen most clearly. It is here that we ought to make a serious start at crossing out the 'I' in our thought and behaviour.

If we each stop to think about our own church, and our part in its life, I suspect we must all admit how far short we fall of this ideal. The next four chapters examine some of the specific areas of church life which would be most radically affected if we could all become less self-centred and more self-denying. The good news is that we can! *The burning and renewing power of the Holy Spirit can do this in you and me.* First, though, we need to ask God to show us where our attitudes are self-centred, bring them to him in repentance, and seek the forgiveness he offers us in Christ.

Shortly before his betrayal and crucifixion, when Jesus washed his disciples' feet, he said he had set them an example. Mutual servanthood was to be the pattern for the communal life of believers. In our relationships with others in Christ's Church, we are not to seek to dominate, coerce or exploit – or, for that matter, ignore them. We are to serve one another in humility. And, said Jesus, 'now that you know these things, you will be blessed if you do them' (John 13:17). The corollary is undoubtedly true: if you do not do them, you will miss out on much of the blessing which should be part of the experience of Christian fellowship.

Attending to the Needs of the Weak

Looking at Jesus proclaiming his kingdom and demonstrating its principles in action, we notice how he appears to concentrate on the weaker or less popular members of the society of his day. He moved among the beggars, the sick, the prostitutes and those despicable men who collected taxes for the occupying Romans – he even chose one of them as a disciple! In fact, he came in for sharp criticism from the church authorities for the people he mixed with. 'Why does he eat with tax collectors and "sinners"?' they asked the disciples, producing from Jesus the response, 'It is not the healthy who need a doctor, but the sick. I have not come to call the righteous, but sinners' (Mark 2:15–17).

What must we learn from this 'bias to the poor' (as it has been called) in Jesus' earthly ministry? It certainly is meant to be emulated, because it is not merely seen in the Gospel stories, but also reflected in the subsequent teaching of the New Testament about the life of his Church. This tells us that, in putting others first, we are urged to pay special attention to the needs not only of those who are materially or socially disadvantaged, but also of those who are 'weak in faith'. Two passages in particular (Rom 14:12–15:4 and 1 Cor 10:23–11:1) expound this principle for the local church. If the idea is unfamiliar to you, it may help to look them up and study them. Both are rooted in the cultural background of the time and place, and the actual issues (such as whether Christians should eat meat previously offered to idols) seem strange to us. They may even appear petty or unimportant – until we stop to think about some of the things we get worked up about, like the raising of hands in worship, or genuflecting towards the altar!

Although the details may be unfamiliar, the principle is clear and uncompromising. However much we may value certain aspects of our own religious practice, where they are likely to be an obstacle to others, the needs of these 'weaker' people are to be given priority. 'Weaker' may mean those with tender consciences, new Christians or those seeking faith.

> We who are strong ought to bear with the failings of the weak and not to please ourselves. Each of us should please his neighbour for his good, to build him up.
>
> (Rom 15:1–2)

> 'Everything is permissible' – but not everything is beneficial. 'Everything is permissible' – but not everything is constructive. Nobody should seek his own good, but the good of others.
>
> For I am not seeking my own good but the good of many, so that they may be saved.
> (1 Cor 10:23–24, 33)

This whole idea may be new to some readers. If so, I hope its impact will become clear when we come to look at one or two examples of how it might operate. The aim of our life together, says Paul, is to build up ('edify') all who are in our fellowship, or for whose spiritual care we are responsible. This must be done with special attention to those most in need of building up.

The Church of England's Rite A Holy Communion service contains a constant reminder of this priority. Before the congregation shares the Peace, the minister reminds us that 'we are the Body of Christ', and exhorts us to 'pursue all that makes for peace and builds up our common life' (Rom 14:19). I try to use this moment for a swift self-examination: have my thoughts and actions towards my fellow-worshippers tended to 'build up', or drag down, the life of the Christian community in which I have a part? I know that at this point in the service some are gritting their teeth for the forthcoming handshake with fellow-worshippers! If they could only relax, and begin to understand the privileges and responsibilities of being 'members together of the Body of Christ', it could be a very constructive moment, re-inforcing the essential un-self-centredness of discipleship. We might not *wish* to be reminded of that at all, let alone regularly; but we certainly all *need* to be.

Learning to Accept Change

The third aspect we noted of Jesus' life and ministry was that meeting him almost invariably proved to be a life-changing experience. Disciples left their daily work and followed him; the sick were healed; unbelievers believed; prostitutes were forgiven and cleaned up their lives; even a cheating tax collector went straight and became an honest philanthropist! (Luke 19:1–10). One of the saddest characters in the Gospels is the rich young man who, unlike almost everyone else who encountered Jesus, went away 'very sad'. He was simply not willing to change his attitude and lifestyle: and it is significant that the change he was unable to embrace involved self-sacrifice (Luke 18:18–25).

Unwillingness to change is also one of the saddest characteristics of church people today. Throughout the Bible God's people are depicted as always on the move, never static. The state of mind needed for this 'pilgrim' existence is the exact opposite of the conservation mentality which has got such a grip on society today – including (perhaps especially!) the Church. To be true to our calling, Christians need to be ready to let go of their past willingly. In saying this, I realise that for some it will automatically discredit anything else I may have to say. But the point is so fundamental, that is a risk I must take!

'Newness' is a central theme running through the entire Bible – a new covenant, a new song, a new heart, a new birth, a new life, a new commandment, a new Jerusalem . . . and, ultimately, a new heaven and a new earth. The promise at the very end of the Bible 'I am making everything new' (Rev 21:5), reveals the direction of the whole of history; while at the personal level, Paul sums up the experience of being 'in Christ' thus: we are 'a new creation; the old has gone, the new has come!' (2 Cor 5:17).

> It is nothing short of tragic that so much church life seems to be concerned with preserving the old, and so much individual energy spent seeking to prevent change.

Church Life – (1) The Sacrificial Pattern

Why should this be? Is it not because many of us are only ready to accept changes which cost us little or nothing? Yet most aspects of change do cost something. Often they involve giving up things which have become dear through familiarity; their loss therefore involves some self-sacrifice, whether corporately or personally. Tracing the history of God's people through the Bible, Maria Boulding points out that for them to follow his call constantly involved being asked to 'let go of a pattern of living which not only meant material security but had been the setting in which they knew his presence'.[2] The letting go was always sacrificial, especially when (as may be the case for us) the thing to be let go of was itself intrinsically good and worthwhile.

> Each time someone ... had been asked to make a leap of faith and love in response to the one who promised, to break through a barrier, to be reborn to a new possibility. The result was a fuller life, a new level and sphere of existence, but at the cost of everything on this side of the barrier. It always meant a letting go, a dying to something that had been familiar, controllable, perhaps even perfect of its kind.[3]

Helen Roseveare, a medical missionary in the 1950s and 60s in the former Congo, gives a down-to-earth example. The palm trees in her village were being stripped by an invasion of weaver birds, ruining the yield of oil vital for both their diet and the local economy. After the village children were offered money for every bird they killed, it was noticed that the lower branches of many other bushes and plants were being destroyed. It turned out that the kids were breaking them off and sharpening them for arrows to shoot at the birds. They were stopped from using branches of coffee, oranges and grapefruit for this purpose, since their fruits too were necessary. But they were allowed to make their weapons from the acacia bushes. With their feathery leaves and bright yellow flowers, these were regarded, especially by white visitors (including herself), as one of the most beautiful local features. In some ways it seemed a wanton act of destruction, a senseless waste of God-given beauty: but in this case the beautiful had to be sacrificed in order to produce the necessary.

To us this example may seem trivial; but in its context it affected the survival of the people and their economy. And, anyway, if we are honest, must we not admit that some of the things we cling on to are pretty unimportant? Reflecting on the lesson of this incident for her own life, Helen Roseveare asked 'Can I see such minor "sacrifices" in the light of the great Sacrifice of Calvary where Christ gave all for me?'[4] That all-important question lies beneath the surface of our many tiny resistances to change.

* * *

Here then are three principles which can be derived from looking at the ministry of Jesus, and to which the rest of the Bible also attests. It is time to get down to brass tacks, and see what might be the result if they were applied prayerfully and thoroughly to life in the Church.

I say '*if*' because, sadly, I have to admit that

Church Life – (1) The Sacrificial Pattern

self-sacrifice does not appear to be the governing principle of much church life, nationally or locally. I say this after much thought, realising that it may sound harsh and judgmental. As I seek in the next four chapters to demonstrate what I mean with reference to various aspects of church life 'as we know it', the tone of some of my remarks may inevitably sound critical – though I hope never negative. So, before we move on, let me hasten, like Paul, to recognise myself as 'the chief of sinners'. I must emphasise that I include myself as the butt of my own criticisms. Where repentance is needed, then (as the old hymn says) 'let it now begin in me'.

FOUR
CHURCH LIFE – (2) WORSHIP

A time . . . has now come when the true worshippers will worship the Father in spirit and truth, for they are the kind of worshippers the Father seeks.

(John 4:23)

Through Jesus, therefore, let us continually offer to God a sacrifice of praise – the fruit of lips that confess his name. And do not forget to do good and to share with others, for with such sacrifices God is pleased.

(Heb 13:15–16)

To many the Sunday services are 'church', and to mess around with them is to challenge the whole identity of their faith and its expression.

(John Leach)[1]

We begin here because for many people going to church is the main, maybe the only, outward expression of their faith. Everyone reading this should be able to identify with it. John 4:23 (above) reminds us that true worship is essentially a spiritual activity. Directed towards God, it is a corporate proclamation of his worth ('worth-ship'), his people consciously offering themselves to him. It is the highest privilege afforded to mankind, the noblest activity in which we can participate. As such it must surely be the area of life where there is least room for self-centredness. Oh dear! After thirty years' involvement in preparing and leading words and music in various churches, I cannot escape the unwelcome conclusion that worship is the area where self-centredness *most* often rears its ugly head. Let me substantiate this.

'I Know What I Like . . .'

In church life, personal tastes are frequently exalted to the status of dogma. Far from putting others first, individuals exert pressure to get what they themselves want. Unable to have their own way, some go off to another church – until the same thing happens again! For others, their whole worshipping life as a church member ceases: one is bound to wonder how much of what Jesus called 'true worship' was ever involved in their churchgoing, if it can simply be turned off like a tap. Still others (far more numerous) stay within the fellowship, but attend only those services which match their personal inclinations: the integrity of the Body and the principle of 'looking to the interests of others' seem to come a poor second to gratifying their own tastes. A last group come to church, but constantly register their likes and dislikes with leaders, maybe underlining their importance by declining to take part in the things they do not like.

> As part of our God-given individuality, our own tastes are important and valuable. I am not suggesting they should be completely suppressed. But 'putting others first' certainly means keeping our preferences in the secondary position where they belong, expressing them appropriately but not seeking to impose them.

After all, to recognise our neighbour's preferences as of *equal* importance to our own is no more than civilised. That is only to reach the starting gate . . . 'even the pagans [today we might say enlightened humanists] do that'. Running the course in a truly Christian (i.e., Christ-like) way will mean going further: 'In humility consider others *better* than yourselves. Each of you should look not only to your own interests, but also to the interests of others' (Phil 2:3-4; italics mine).

Years ago, as a 'traditional' church musician, I reacted with distaste and dismay to 'inferior and repetitive choruses' and twanging guitars. As this upstart culture increasingly disrupted the comfortable 'organ and choir' nest I had helped build, matters came to a head. Unable to reconcile the high standards sought (sometimes even achieved!) in the choir's music with the 'anything goes' approach to choruses, I insisted on being made responsible for the whole lot. The implications dawned only slowly. If I was to nurture in others the idea that 'only the best is good enough for God' – a phrase frequently used by traditionalists to defend their own tastes – I personally must be seen to put as much care and effort into what I initially regarded as 'inferior' music as I did in the more 'exalted' repertoire. I began to recognise that many worshippers found in these new, simple songs a valuable medium for expressing their devotion to God. If God could use this music to deepen his people's worshipping lives, I had no business to regard it as 'inferior'. (Note, though, that there are intrinsically good and bad examples – but there are in traditional music too!). So I started – unwillingly at first, since it involved denying my own tastes at the time – to apply to it such gifts as God has given me, and encourage others to do so. This proved a blessing both to those I tried to serve and (to my surprise) to myself. In time, this period proved to have been a training ground for a much wider music ministry. The Holy Spirit was, and is, changing God's people. Becoming aware of this, and learning to accept it, resulted in being changed myself in unlooked-for ways, which have brought great blessing. To God be the glory!

The 'Weaker Members'

As we saw in the previous chapter, the discipline of self-sacrifice is concerned not only with our own spiritual growth, but also the interests of those needing to be 'built up'. In relation to worship this is frequently overlooked. It is so important that we should consider a number of examples.

Those of us brought up on the Church of England's traditional liturgy can fail to realise how difficult some people find it. For those from other churches, or no church background at all, it is unfamiliar or culturally irrelevant, a medium through which they simply cannot validly express their own worship. The same may be true for those without the advantages of a good education. In some respects they may actually be 'stronger' Christians than ourselves; but finding themselves disadvantaged in worship they are in this particular way 'weaker'. Are their needs being considered when self-interest causes PCCs to retain services conceived in and for the world of centuries ago?

We similarly under-estimate the difficulty youngsters, or adults not brought up in churchgoing families, have in understanding many Bible passages read in the (to them) completely unfamiliar idiom of the Authorised Version. When readers insist on using it because they like the beauty of its language, what thought are they giving to these others? Do they consider their own responsibility for 'building up the Body', in which reading and hearing the word of God play a vital part?

Some preachers (especially among evangelicals!) habitually make allusions ('. . . as you will remember from the story of Mephibosheth . . .') which mean nothing to their congregation. I am sure they are not parading their own knowledge; but it is legitimate to ask whether they stop to think how this makes hearers feel inadequate or excluded. That approach may have been appropriate to an era when the majority of a congregation had a good Bible knowledge. But that is very far from being the norm today; preachers should deny themselves the ease of such long-outdated assumptions.

Sometimes, of course, the boot is on the other foot. The 'modernisers' may need to recognise as 'weaker brethren' those who find overt displays of enthusiasm disturbing. The freedom to clap or raise our hands must similarly be exercised with due regard to its effect on others. Insensitivity or arrogance on the part of those claiming to have

Church Life – (2) Worship

been renewed by the Spirit in their worship is even harder to understand than the inhibitions of those making no such claim. Watching some worshipping with their eyes tightly shut, I am sometimes anxious that the 'renewal culture' tends to encourage unhealthy individualism. 'I'll shut others out while I have a great time with God.' (Hearing people say '*I* pray . . .' in public prayer causes me the same anxiety.) Authentic signs of renewal are a *greater* awareness of our fellow-worshippers, *greater* sensitivity to one another, and *greater* concern for our *corporate* worship to be acceptable to God.

Lastly, a quite different kind of example. Some congregations include people who have, or are overcoming, serious alcohol problems. What should be done about the wine at Communion? There is a risk that what ought to be a means of deepening faith might become, for these 'weaker' members, their downfall. The 'weaker brother' principle would seem to suggest using something non-alcoholic. How would you react to that? (If you think this somewhat far-fetched, let me assure you that it was a real issue in the church where I served until recently.[2])

Putting Ourselves into it

In the verses from Hebrews at the head of this chapter, the writer uses the significant phrase 'the *sacrifice* of praise'. This is indissolubly linked with the sacrifice of right living, both in this text and consistently throughout the Old and New Testaments (e.g. 1 Sam 15:22; Amos 5:21–24; Matt 5:23–24). The two aspects are clearly inter-dependent: neither, without the other, is acceptable to

God. But it is certainly true that 'recovering this notion of the sacrifice of praise ... is vital to the reinvigoration of Christian worship ... and fundamental to the renewal of the Church'.[3] In worship, the two strands of what 'sacrifice' means (giving ourselves up, and making holy) come together particularly clearly. The sacrificial element arises not only from considerations of putting others first, but from what it *costs* us in other ways – time, energy, concentration and toleration. The cost may also include being willing to lower the barriers behind which we feel secure, and to relinquish cherished things. One of the Iona liturgies uses the phrase, 'We will not offer to the Lord offerings that cost us nothing'.[4]

In practice, our level of *personal commitment* to worship when we arrive at church is often so low that we have (as contemporary worship leader Graham Kendrick puts it) to be 'bump-started', like a faulty car engine! How much do we actually put into worship? The question may sound strange to our ears. Perhaps we are more likely to ask, 'how much do I get out of it?'. If so, this probably indicates that we regard a church service as something done by others for our benefit – failing to realise that it is, in fact, a corporate act which we must each as an individual worshipper help to create.

Our failure to put much of ourselves into an act of worship may, of course, be precisely because it is not the sort of service we like. But 'mature Christians are those who have discovered the value of giving worship to God in spite of their feelings as well as because of them.'[5] I would add from personal experience that it is particularly when we do have to put ourselves out, in order to put ourselves into it, that God delights in our worship

Church Life – (2) Worship

and often blesses us richly through it, precisely because it *is* sacrificial. So don't criticise the sermons while neglecting to pray for the preacher. Don't say the singing is bad, while making only a dull and listless contribution yourself. Don't talk about the importance of fellowship, yet scuttle hastily into church just as the service begins.

> It is not everyone else's responsibility to get the church's worshipping life right so that you can enjoy it: it is what you bring that counts.

As John Leach says:

> We wait for the worship to become good before we give ourselves to it, rather than diving in and making it good. That *sacrifice of praise* – putting ourselves out no matter how we feel – simply because God is worth it, is something which the Bible demands of us.[6]

The Fringe

All churches, regardless of size, have people who appear from time to time – at weddings and funerals, or as visitors. Even regular attenders always include some who are there out of convention or habit rather than personal Christian conviction. Some youngsters may be there under parental pressure – conversely, some adults because they come with their children. Others are seeking or moving towards faith. Some might come for the music, or the companionship. To describe these heterogeneous folk as 'fringe' is in no way meant to sound patronising. It is not even mathematically accurate – since they can account for over half of some congregations. They are 'fringe' only in that their understanding of, or commitment to, the Christian faith is as yet undeveloped. Ministering to them poses perhaps the greatest sacrificial challenge to the faithful. At least some – let us say a significant proportion – of what we do should aim to *include* rather than *exclude* them.

The points already made apply with even greater force in regard to such folk. They need to hear the Bible in language they can understand. We owe them biblically-based preaching which contains the essence and challenge of the gospel expressed in terms which are relevant to their lives. And let us try to look at the rest of our worship through their eyes. I must not be diverted into too much detail; but consider the following:

> We acknowledge and bewail our manifold sins and wickedness, Which we, from time to time, most grievously have committed, By thought, word, and deed, Against thy Divine Majesty, Provoking most justly thy wrath and indignation against us. We do earnestly repent, And are heartily sorry for these our misdoings; The remembrance of them is grievous unto us; The burden of them is intolerable . . .
> (Holy Communion, Book of Common Prayer)

> Almighty God, our heavenly Father,
> we have sinned against you and against our
>   fellow men,
> in thought and word and deed,
> through negligence, through weakness,
> through our own deliberate fault.

> We are truly sorry,
> and repent of all our sins.
>
> (Holy Communion Rite A,
> Alternative Service Book)

Which of these is more likely to help such people to become aware that their lives fall short of what God intends and requires? Which will enable them to express this awareness in terms valid *for them*, and to seek forgiveness sincerely? Can those with a strong streak of conservatism not make the small sacrifice involved 'in order to save some'? Such examples could be multiplied.

What about the things we ask people to sing. Recently I and six other worshippers had to ask ourselves (to an impossibly dreary tune) whether we were 'weary, languid and sore distrest', and, if we were to find One (unnamed) 'what his guerdon here?'. Even I (seasoned campaigner that I am!) felt stupid. Of course we must cherish the great treasures of the past. But it is not just today's worship material which quickly becomes dated. Much of yesterday's material dated decades ago! We seriously fail worshippers by giving them the second-rate of yesterday, while ignoring today's new hymns and songs (some of them first-rate). Nor are modern worship songs off the hook. Some are esoteric, with phrases like 'Pierce my ear', or frankly ridiculous, with lines like 'Lord, you put some hands on my arms'. And we cannot afford to ignore the *double-entendres* which sadly mar some worship songs: they are bound to have the opposite effect than that intended on a mixed congregation in our sex-obsessed society. Even with good-quality material, those leading worship or choosing music may on occasions have to restrain their own inclinations, and mature worshippers make their own sacrifice. People 'on the fringe' are unlikely to be helped by stringing together ten minutes of devotional songs expressing personal love and worship, which they cannot sing with integrity.

It is vital to recognise that those who stand to lose most are people who are unable to express themselves sincerely in the worship material we use. This may be because it is full of Christian 'jargon', redolent of a Christian past they do not share, or makes them snigger. The principle is that 'we who are strong ought . . . not to please ourselves. Each of us should please his neighbour . . . to build him up' (Rom 15:1–2).

> Meeting the needs of the weak, without impoverishing the strong and mature, is a balancing act. Do pray for your worship leaders rather than criticising them.

The 'Geography' of Worship

Our buildings are another aspect where we may need to think more sacrificially, particularly about the extent to which they help or hinder our awareness of ourselves as 'members together of Christ's Body' as we gather to worship. A couple of examples may help to show what I mean.

John Leach again: 'In the past, worship was often seen as a very individualistic and private matter . . . one regarded one's fellow-worshippers as intruders rather than as valued companions (and often glared at them accordingly!).'[7]

There are still those who see worship as a private matter, and restrict their churchgoing largely

Church Life – (2) Worship

to an early morning Communion service. But most Christians now recognise that interaction is a vital ingredient of worship. We are, after all, exhorted to address and encourage *one another* as we lift our praise to God (Eph 5:19; Col 3:16). It is not easy to interact with the back of someone's head! The serried rows of pews we regard as normal have done more than any other single factor to bolster the idea of worship as a spectator event, 'done' by those up the front for the benefit of those in the 'auditorium'. That is death to truly communal worship. Some have grasped this nettle. A formerly redundant Cambridge church has recently re-opened, with seating facing inwards across the central aisle. Even a semi-circular arrangement of chairs greatly assists worshippers' awareness of one another, as we discovered when I worked at St John's, Boscombe in Bournemouth. But how many congregations would be willing to make such changes (supposing the powers that be allowed them to)? Even where our buildings and their contents are of no special artistic merit or historic interest, their very age mostly overrides considerations of lively worship appropriate to today's needs. Too often we are simply not prepared to sacrifice the baggage of past centuries.

The traditional layout of most churches means that the action at Holy Communion services disappears into the middle distance just as the most visually important moment approaches. This belongs to an age which thought it appropriate for the 'holy mysteries' to be celebrated almost out of sight and hearing of the ignorant laity. The nave, chancel and sanctuary set-up in most Anglican buildings – including those built since the Reformation – still reflects the priestly worship of the Old Testament rather than the gathering of God's people (*ekklesia*) in the New Testament. And all this despite Archbishop Cranmer's prescription in the sixteenth century that the table should be brought down and placed in the congregation. Today Christians recognise that

> God . . . takes delight in holy people – those who have been made glad by the assurance of sins forgiven, and strong in the knowledge of a love and power beyond their own. The means by which these benefits come to them are not appropriately 'done in a corner', enacted behind a stone or wooden screen . . . they are to be openly proclaimed, placarded with joy in the midst of the congregation, 'showing forth the Lord's death, till he come'.[8]

Yet so many church people are aghast at the very thought of re-ordering church buildings. They are unable to contemplate the sacrificial cost in terms either of finance or the loss of the familiar. Consequently, worship so often gets locked in to the past, and fails to reflect contemporary insights into the nature of the people of God.

The 'Un-churched' – Daring to Think Big

We shall be looking at the Church's evangelistic task in Chapter Six. In any event I do not believe (although this is not a subject I can pursue here) that worship is *primarily* about evangelism.

Church Life – (2) Worship

Nevertheless, in making contact with our non-Christian neighbours, it is natural and right to want to be able to invite them to church with us. So, before leaving the subject of worship, we must consider it in relation to non-members. Here we come up against a problem more desperate than any that has faced the Church for many previous generations.

The phrase 'the un-churched' may well be new to many readers. It is not meant (like 'the great unwashed'!) to sound disparaging. In fact it describes a new phenomenon which ought perhaps to be regarded as the product of our own failure. In Britain we now have the first adult generation who know nothing whatsoever about Christianity. It is not necessarily that they have rejected, or even ignored, it. They have literally never heard anything about it – not from their parents, who were the kids of the 1960s and 70s; not from their school assemblies which, if they happened at all, were devoid of any Christian content; not by the most casual contact with the Church, which they regard as totally irrelevant. And we are not talking here of an uneducated minority.

> A survey of Oxbridge undergraduates a few years ago found an alarming proportion who did not know which came first, the crucifixion or the resurrection!

Yes . . . these kids are now growing up and giving birth to a second un-churched generation.

How many of us are even aware of this situation? How many can see that this is not something we can shrug off; it is *our* problem? How many will think about the implications? How many are prepared to take costly action to address them? The answer to each question gets smaller. But there are some taking it seriously. A number of British churches are setting out to provide 'churches for the un-churched', and resources and materials are becoming available to help others do likewise.[9] These activities aim to start from where un-churched people are, and to present the gospel to them in a way which assumes no knowledge, takes place in a non-threatening environment and aims to 'make disciples of all'.

Often (though not always) such initiatives are associated with 'church planting'. Here a number of Christians from an existing church set up a new embryo congregation in an area where the gospel seems to have failed to penetrate, and work to grow a new church through 'seeker-orientated' worship and other activities. This can be very costly, both for the 'mother church' which loses some of its most confident and gifted members, and for those who go into the new situation, leaving behind the environment of a thriving church and strong fellowship to be pioneers for the gospel's sake.

Because it *is* very costly, it is also very Christ-like. It is truly 'living for others'. No doubt that is why George Carey, soon after becoming Archbishop of Canterbury, said every church should aim to plant another. That must be regarded as an ambitious, long-term, aim. But there are plenty of vigorous churches who could be considering both church planting and re-organising their own life to make specific efforts to reach the un-churched, and who are not yet doing so. Smaller churches are unlikely to have the resources for any spectacular new initiatives; but they must at least begin to address their responsibility to the

Church Life – (2) Worship

complete outsider. A good starting point would be to ask: 'Is there *any* part of our life and activities directed specifically to the un-churched?' They might then go on to ask, 'How far is what we do *accessible* to complete outsiders? What is the impact on them of taking collections, unexplained rituals, boring sermons, hostility towards children . . . ?'

Facing up to Change

Most of these issues and examples bring us sharply up against the third principle identified in Chapter Three – the need to accept change. As we noted, Christians are an essentially pilgrim people, who recognise that here we do not have an 'enduring city' but are 'looking for the city that is to come' (Heb 13:14). Change *ought* not to be difficult for us. Yet experience suggests the very opposite. John Leach (who ministered in a church pioneering 'seeker' events) recognises that changing worship patterns does cause real difficulties for 'old-stagers'; but proper concern for them must be balanced by our responsibility to those not 'in the know':

> First, we have a God-given responsibility towards those for whom we have pastoral care in the congregation . . . We have to love them and strive with the Spirit to present them mature and spotless to the Father. But we also have a responsibility to those outside the church, to win them to faith in the Lord. Sometimes these two responsibilities conflict when those in the church seem determined, by their conservatism and intransigence, to

keep the outsiders outside by maintaining the church in a state of terminal irrelevance. It is our job . . . to work out these two areas of responsibility, but if at times we leave behind those inside, that may be a necessary evil in order to fulfil our responsibility to those outside.[10]

Many congregations recognise themselves as a sad, ageing, dwindling and often rather dis-spirited minority. Like the rich young ruler, they come to church and 'go away sad', unwilling to face the cost of sacrificing the familiar and the time-honoured in order to venture into the unknown. At almost every turn they opt for the *status quo*, the things with which they feel secure. This may not be recognised for the self-centredness which it undoubtedly is. In fact it is nothing less than tragic. As Ian Bradley says: 'Unless the Church as Christ's body itself more clearly bears the marks of suffering and the scars of sacrifice, it is hard to see how anyone will take its message seriously.'[11]

For those with eyes to see, there are signs of awakening and renewal in the Church, and potential for real growth. At the same time, those churches whose life is in a downward spiral continue to resist the very changes which could bring new life to them. It is increasingly difficult to see how many of them can survive much longer.

> There are some places, particularly in country areas, where a recognizable, worshipping Christian community may soon disappear altogether.

If that happens, I fear church people will place the blame everywhere except where it belongs – that

Church Life – (2) Worship

is, with their own unwillingness to sacrifice their comfort and security for the sake of this and future generations. Maria Boulding, although writing in a slightly different context, nevertheless sums this up in a telling way:

> Old patterns break . . . growth often proceeds in jumps. The moments of breakthrough can be ruthlessly demanding. If the demand is refused, we do not merely continue at the old level, but shrink and shrivel into death; so we lose what we had in any case. It is an exhausting business for the tiny chicken to chip its way out of the egg, but the alternative is worse.[12]

FIVE

CHURCH LIFE – (3) RELATIONSHIPS

... in Christ we who are many form one body, and each member belongs to all the others.
(Rom 12:5)

Once a congregation grasps that God has called us collectively as his people so that his glory might be seen in us, that congregation may well be transformed.

(David Watson)[1]

After we moved home recently, friends asked, 'Have you found a good church?' What *is* a 'good' church? As a teenager my answer would have been 'one with a good organ'. That would subsequently have broadened into 'one with good music'. A little later, having been nourished in the evangelical tradition, I should have focussed on 'sound preaching'; then that expanded to include 'where the worship is lively'. Nowadays, though, any definition I might attempt of a 'good' church would major on the quality of its relationships.

In practice, factors like these are mutually dependent. Good quality music (of all styles) helps make lively worship; good biblical preaching tends

Church Life – (3) Relationships

to build up a congregation's life; a 'lively' congregation is likely to express itself in good worship . . . and so on. In that sense, it is unprofitable to try to separate them. But what I believe is important – because it signals our own growth as Christians – is to see some *progress* in our perceptions of what makes a 'good' church. For my own Christian 'growth record', charted above, I have entirely to thank God and the godly leaders he has given me. I believe it is typical of the way God works in our lives. There is a discernible progress from:

- what concerns our own particular interests or gifts (for me it was music, though other things may have mattered more to you); through

- things that reflect the particular Christian tradition in which we feel at home, making us regard a 'good' church as one whose worship displays the characteristics with which we are familiar and comfortable; to

- the realisation that 'the Church' is about so much more than what goes on inside its doors on a Sunday – in fact it is about being the Body of Christ.

You may have learnt the old mnemonic as a child:

Jesus first
Others next
Yourself last

spells JOY. Really smart readers may have noticed that the course I have just outlined marks a change in outlook on your church from **Y** (your own personal interests), through **O** (the tradition which you share with, and is approved by, others) to **J** (Jesus as the Head of his Body, the Church): YOJ, in fact! I believe the desire in God's heart, and the work of his Spirit in our lives, is to transform us from **YOJ**ful people into **JOY**ful people. That transformation, the promotion of Jesus from last place to first, and the demotion of self from first place to last, is what John the Baptist was talking about when he said 'He [Jesus] must become greater; I must become less' (John 3:30). It is, in fact, the life of growing self-sacrifice, the way of the Cross.

Having looked at some of the issues which arise concerning worship, I now turn to some of the ways in which congregational life would be vitally changed by applying sacrificial principles to our relationships with each other.

Loving One Another

Jesus gave his disciples a 'new commandment', that they should love one another. To remove any doubt about what he meant, he qualified it . . . 'as I have loved you'. Still room for misunderstanding? He spelt out even more plainly that he was talking about a quality of love which would mean willingness to lay down their life for one another. Did he lay this on them as a burden, or a hard test of their commitment? No . . . 'I have told you this so that my joy may be in you *and that your joy may be complete*' (John 15:9–17; italics mine). Surprising as it may seem at first

Church Life – (3) Relationships

sight, the way of self-sacrifice is a way of joy. In Christian relationships, in particular, it is the work of Satan to persuade us that the opposite is true, that happiness comes from defending our own interests. This is, as we saw in Chapter One, the Original Lie. Ian Bradley writes that 'it is through acts of self-giving, mercy and compassion that we can be freed from the tyranny of self. . . . Sacrifice thus becomes the basis for human happiness and fulfilment.'[2] Until we understand and believe that, we shall always be inclined to hold back.

It was said of the early Church, 'See how these Christians love one another.' Obviously they were putting Christ's new commandment into practice, and it made some impact. But then it would, because it is so different from the way in which the world handles relationships. We can see this where Paul spells out what 'love one another' means in a Christian congregation:

> Therefore, as God's chosen people, holy and dearly loved, clothe yourselves with compassion, kindness, humility, gentleness and patience. Bear with each other and forgive whatever grievances you may have against one another. Forgive as the Lord forgave you. And over all these virtues put on love, which binds them all together in perfect unity.
>
> (Col 3:12–14)

This is the clearest, and probably the most challenging, picture in the Bible of what church life ought to be like. Mutual forbearance and forgiveness are at its heart, love binds it all together . . .

the undemanding, self-giving love exemplified by Jesus on the cross. This love is (writes Herbert Carson), 'the life blood of the other virtues. Without love they are only dutiful moral attitudes, but with love they are blended into a moral unity which is complete. Completeness would also suggest . . . being acceptable to God.'[3] It makes all the other virtues acceptable precisely because, bonded by self-giving love, they become sacrificial.

It has been borne in on me over the years how frequently bad relationships spoil the life of congregations. I do not mean only failure to 'honour one another above yourselves' (Rom 12:10), but unforgiveness – active harbouring of grudges against one another. Usually they began over some trifling incident, or supposed slight; but over time they have been clung on to, even carefully nurtured. This kind of long-term unforgiveness is highly dangerous. Christ himself spoke about the link between God's forgiveness of us and our willingness to forgive others (Matt 6:14–15). This is a very solemn truth. It ought to challenge us every single time we say the Lord's Prayer – unless we are completely on 'automatic pilot'.

It is vital to realise that this is not just a matter between ourself and the other person. One of Protestantism's weaknesses has been to encourage an individualistic approach to faith and practice which seriously under-estimates the effect of each individual's actions on the whole Body. 'If one part suffers, every part suffers with it' (1 Cor 12:26). This applies even to our presence or absence at services: if only Christians would realise that, by staying away voluntarily from a service, they impoverish the whole Body. (A mature Christian

Church Life – (3) Relationships

once walked out of a choir practice before I had even finished the opening prayer – and never came back – because I implied this.) That is why the early Christians were exhorted not to give up meeting together, as some were doing, but to encourage one another. Regular fellowship and mutual encouragement are not optional, but essential, if a Christian community is to be built up. And if our very presence or absence has an effect on others, how much more so the frame of mind in which we come. Do you realise that your own attitude to your fellow-worshippers, the music, the preacher, actually affects everybody else? This is a sobering thought, but absolutely true: 'Each member belongs to all the others' (Rom 12:5).

Thus Michael Marshall writes: 'So I am my brother's keeper and both my evil deeds as well as my faith affect others. God's people have in that sense always been . . . men and women for others, not individualists just for themselves.'[4]

> Broken relationships between church members affect the flow of God's grace and blessing not just to themselves, but to others. The poison can spread right through a congregation.

Christ told his followers to 'be reconciled to your brother' before coming to the altar. This is, incidentally, another very positive and practical way to use the 'Peace' at the Holy Communion: it affords an opportunity to make good any broken relationships, quite privately but before the Lord. (I once did this without realising my radio microphone was still on!) To meet someone's eyes while wishing them the 'peace of the Lord' leaves little room for harbouring bitterness. Dietrich Bonhoeffer writes:

> If we despise our brother our worship is unreal, and it forfeits every divine promise . . . So long as we refuse to love and serve our brother . . . and let him harbour a grudge against me or the congregation, our worship and sacrifice will be unacceptable to God. Not just the fact that I am angry, but the fact that there is somebody who has been hurt . . . erects a barrier between me and God.[5]

Harbouring wrong attitudes – envy, contempt, spite, anger, and especially unforgiveness – towards fellow-members is putting the capital 'I' right at the centre, and keeping it there. It is self-importance at its worst. And because these attitudes affect the rest of Christ's Body, holding on to them is self-indulgence at its most spiritually dangerous. It has no place in the life of the disciple. Conversely, 'Consider the healing power of real forgiveness, one of the most difficult and costly forms of sacrifice, which can blot out long-harboured resentments and bitterness both in individuals and communities'.[6]

Such forgiveness can, likewise, have a positive effect that spreads far beyond the individuals concerned in a fellowship.

Working Together

> No body would function properly if many of its organs took little or no part in the well-being

of the whole. The Church's . . . effectiveness
depends upon the prayers and work of every
member . . . The call to be a Christian and
to follow Christ is not just a call to ally
oneself with a group of people who hold
certain views and meet together in a formal
way on Sundays. It is a call which involves
a *call-up* to wholehearted service for all who
claim the name of 'Christian'. Neither the
plain teaching of the New Testament nor the
desperate needs of today can possibly allow
any other conclusion.[7]

Some readers may be thinking 'what's he on
about now?'. Maybe you do not see the connection
between your church membership and 'work'. You
have a vicar or minister to do the church's work
– conducting services and visiting people – that's
what he or she is paid for, isn't it? They, and
possibly one or two helpers, do the work . . . your
role is to 'support' them by going to their services.
That may sound like a caricature; but it really is
how many churchgoers regard their membership.
Anyway, apart from attending services, what else
is there to do? In a very small church, this may
almost be true. But ask yourself this question: if
that is all you can think of to do, is that perhaps
why yours is a very small church? A congregation
with any vision of its role in the world will never
be short of things to do.

But 'the plain fact is that the exercise of our
gifts in the service of Christ actively involves only
a small proportion of members in only a small
proportion of churches'.[8] Those words, written in
1973, sadly remain true today. Even in churches
which are up-and-doing, where there is obviously

work to be done, the majority often behave more like passengers on a cruise-liner than the crew of a lifeboat! There are a number of common reasons for this:

- They genuinely believe they do not have any gifts. They are almost always mistaken. The New Testament teaches that gifts, whether particular ministries, the so-called 'spiritual gifts' or 'gifts of service', are shared amongst all God's people. (See, for example, 1 Peter 4:10–11 and Ephesians 4:7.) Such people need to be taught and encouraged by the leaders to explore their gifts and how they can be of service to God and his people.

- The minister does not seek to involve members in the church's work, either because he thinks he is the only one capable of doing most things or he feels threatened by the abilities of others. (I say 'he' because observation suggests that men in leadership are much more prone to this than women.) This is not the pattern of the living Body of Christ. In this case would-be-active members need to encourage their minister to face up to the challenges and enormous potential of 'every-member ministry'. (Yes, I know – it's not easy this way round!)

- Members recognise that there is much work to be done, and know their contribution would be welcomed. But even where their circumstances would allow them to do so, they do not get involved, because it would be costly; they cannot 'afford' the time or effort it would take.

Church Life – (3) Relationships

The first two, which are common and important, merit a book on their own ... but this is not it! We must address the third.

> It is a sad fact that many people in churches large and small throughout the land see their church as there to serve them, rather than as a means of grace through which they themselves can serve God.

It is not surprising if, with this outlook, they take what they can get out of their membership without putting anything much into it. This has two undesirable results. Obviously it limits the amount of work that can be done. It also places the comparatively few really dedicated members, and maybe their families too, under great stress. Of course, the demands of full-time work, family, other community activities – and adequate leisure – are important. No one, including God, is well-served by neglecting these in order to be at church meetings every night of the week. But if only enough members made their own contribution to the church's life, there would be no need for the few to burn themselves out. This is not an appeal for people to make a special effort. We are all expected to *do* something as a result of our faith. James, warning us against hearing the word of God but not doing what it says, exhorts us to the practicalities of 'true religion' (Js 1:22–27), and sums it all up succinctly: 'Faith without deeds is dead' (Js 2:26). Paul adds: 'Always give yourself fully to the work of the Lord, because you know that your labour in the Lord is not in vain' (1 Cor 15:58).

Paul also writes that our 'reasonable service' to God involves offering our bodies (i.e., our whole human selves) as a 'living sacrifice' (Rom 12:1). Whatever form our service may take, it begins to be acceptable to God only when it costs something. Doing God's work only if it is convenient, or not too demanding of time or effort, falls far short of the New Testament picture of discipleship . . . in particular of Christ's call to deny ourselves and take up our cross daily.

Of course there are some who simply cannot offer much time or energy – it may be for reasons of health, circumstances or the constraint of a non-Christian partner. Such people should not feel a sense of failure or guilt: any service they can offer is, like the widow's mite (Luke 21:1–4), truly sacrificial – not only acceptable but praiseworthy. Others, who are very new in Christian faith, may take some time to understand either the principles or the need for sacrificial service to God and others. (Occasionally the opposite occurs: leaders have to cope with brand new Christians full of the 'joy of the Lord' who believe they can do everything immediately, and cannot accept any kind of restraint.)

Experience suggests that the real untapped reservoir of Christian workers lies in those who profess faith, but have not yet really appreciated the wonder of belonging to God or the debt they owe him. They are rarely moved by appeals for help. Leaders must concentrate on seeking to open up these people to the wonder of God's love, through preaching, teaching, individual pastoral work and persevering prayer. A commitment to faithful, sacrificial service must spring not just from a sense of duty to the church, but of gratitude to God. 'How can I repay the LORD for all his goodness to me?' (Ps 116:12). Achieving this response requires patience rather than pressure!

Church Life – (3) Relationships

On the other hand, it is all too easy for people to grow in faith and knowledge of God without a corresponding growth in awareness of their responsibility to others (inside and outside the Church) and commitment to God's service. Nobody's interests are served by allowing growing Christians to adopt the 'pew fodder' mentality. The wise pastor will seek God's grace to spot where this is happening and to issue a gentle challenge. This might be done by exploring together what gifts the people concerned may have, and how they could best be used. General appeals or edicts in this area will not work. It will have to be on a one-to-one basis, or perhaps in a small group. All very time-consuming for the busy leader; but it is (as we shall see in Chapter Seven) the very stuff of Christian leadership to stimulate growth, not only in faith and understanding, but in committed, self-sacrificing discipleship.

On the whole, I believe it is high time for many of us Christians to review our expectations of church membership, to examine the balance between giving and receiving, and return in penitence to the Lord who himself 'did not come to be served, but to serve' (Matt 20:28).

* * *

There is a challenge also for those of us who may feel we have identified our gifts and put them at the disposal of God and his church. Even this can be done in a spirit of either self-fulfilment or self-sacrifice. David Prior writes:

> I can easily see the life of the Church as providing me with an opportunity to exercise

> my gifts and to find personal fulfilment. If I
> am prevented for whatever reason from thus
> expressing myself freely, I become impatient
> and crotchety. The spirit of servanthood . . .
> involves looking for opportunities to attend
> to the needs of my fellow Christians, rather
> than scope for my gifts.[9]

At the everyday level, this can be a problem with 'natural talents'. In the last church where I was Director of Music, one gifted teenager had the talent both to sing bass and play the trumpet (though not at the same time!). The former was what we urgently *needed* just then; but the latter was what he *wanted* to do. He too 'went away sad', because he was (at that time) unwilling to sacrifice his desire for self-fulfilment.

The same can apply to the holding of office or responsibility in the church, and (for those who regard 'spiritual' gifts as a separate category) the exercise of such gifts. You might be carrying out your ministry effectively and with real dedication. It may involve genuine sacrifice of time, effort and emotional or physical stamina. That is all excellent, of course. Tribute should be paid to those who have given themselves selflessly to their church's work for years: there are churches which owe their very existence to such people's costly commitment. We should never take them for granted. But this should not blind us to the fact that others have clung on to some work or office, maybe because they rely on it for their status or self-worth, or perhaps in the belief that nobody else could do it so well.

One test of the balance between self-fulfilment and self-sacrifice in our Christian service might be to ask ourselves how we should react if it was suggested we should give up the work we are doing. It might be because changes in our church's life mean our particular ministry is no longer called for. We may have been doing it for so long that a fresh approach is needed. Perhaps our elders can see that, for our own good, we need to be less active. Or maybe (here's the crunch!) someone else in the church has similar gifts or potential which need to be developed, and the only way for this to be achieved is for us to stand aside. How would we feel then? To accept it graciously would certainly be an indication of putting others first. To be able to accept it gladly, rejoicing that God is continuing to 'build up the Body', would be a real mark of the Holy Spirit at work in our life. And it would be a powerful testimony to others which would further build up the Church.

Making Decisions Together

The mechanics of 'church government' vary greatly. The historic denominations tend to be centralised and slow. The weight of bureaucracy and checks and balances (and the paperwork to go with them!) which the Church of England drags with it – largely by virtue of its Establishment – is appalling. In most Nonconformist churches more responsibility rests with the local congregation for its own government. This is especially true of the new and more volatile 'house churches', where the decision process is often largely a matter for individual leaders.

But the question I want to highlight is this:

whatever the structure within which a local church operates, can decisions be made which rely on individuals adopting a sacrificial attitude? Or – to put it another way – does the local leadership have to be content with whatever can be achieved through 'consensus politics', or without upsetting certain individuals? Is it a case of 'we couldn't possibly change the service times, because Mrs X wouldn't like it . . .': and Mrs X is a force to be reckoned with because she's the daughter of the Dowager Duchess of Wintonshire? We can't have a Family Communion because it would go against the grain with Mr Y, and look how much he gives to the church's funds. We can't replace those worn-out frontals until Mrs Z dies, because her father donated them in 1910. We can't have the robed choir at the Family Service, because the Music Group leader would resign. And vice versa at the Eucharist, of course! These are not tongue-in-cheek examples: they all happen . . . regularly!

> As a member of a church, how do you seek to influence its life? Do you go to the Church Meeting merely to press your own viewpoint? Or do you listen attentively and prayerfully to others, trying to discern God's will and the needs of the Body?

Most traditions have some kind of election process for leaders and officers. Since the introduction of synodical government in the Church of England, the Parochial Church Council is the bottom tier of a four-storey edifice, with Deanery, Diocesan and General Synods above it (although, as I write, these structures are under review). The enormous (and, I

Church Life – (3) Relationships

agree, necessary) paraphernalia of elections, voting procedures, and references up and down, reflect our parliamentary democracy. Most English people regard this as the only decent way to organise anything! It is true that this opened up the decision-making process to ordinary lay members – which was long overdue. The trouble is that, when all is said and done, I am not sure that God's Church is *meant* to be a democracy.

Returning to the Body metaphor, the essential factor is that Christ himself is the Head: 'And he [Christ] is the head of the body, the church; he is the beginning and the firstborn from among the dead, so that in everything he might have the supremacy' (Col 1:18). What does this mean for the question we are considering? We saw in Chapter Three how it is no accident that Christ's *body*, in which he expressed the ultimate self-sacrifice, was given as the metaphor for his Church. We should expect, then, that his Headship of the Body will express itself in sacrificial actions throughout its members. Only in that way will they be truly 'joined to' the Head. Paul spells this out in relation to the unity of God's people:

> . . . speaking the truth in love, we will in all things grow up into him who is the Head, that is, Christ. From him the whole body, joined and held together by every supporting ligament, grows and builds itself up in love, as each part does its work.
>
> (Eph 4:15–16)

He was not suggesting – neither am I – a congregation of docile 'doormats' who just do what

they are told. Far from it. He implies in these
verses:

- *communication*, where truth is always tempered by love;
- *growth* as both a vital concern and an expectation;
- *unity* arising from the separate parts being controlled by the one Head;
- *work* as the means through which God's purpose is achieved through the Body.

I believe God's will for any church is discovered only when the members' insights and aspirations are brought together, discussed openly, weighed up to see how they contribute to the building up of the Body, prayed over ... and sometimes, if necessary to achieve a unity of purpose, left to lie for a while. Then, when a decision is arrived at, it is to be accepted and worked for by everyone, including those whose own wishes have not been accommodated by it. In a political democracy, we all know that, whatever the theory, in practice the minority continue to campaign and act in a generally negative or disruptive way. *This pattern from the world simply must not be accepted as the way God's Church works.* There is no place in Christ's kingdom for His Majesty's Opposition! None of us can have things all our own way in church life.

We ought to be able to see this simply by thinking clearly about our position in *the Body*; failing that, by considering our relationship with Christ as *the Head*. Both aspects come together in

Church Life – (3) Relationships

a verse which ought to be recited together every time Christians meet to plan or discuss congregational life: 'Submit to one another out of reverence for Christ' (Eph 5:21). If we cannot accept this principle, either for the good of the Body or the honour of Christ, we need to turn again to the cross of Calvary – or maybe go there in true repentance for the first time. There, in the light of the ultimate sacrifice Jesus made for our good and God's honour, we must pray for forgiveness and grace.

Giving

Those who thought a book about living sacrificially must be primarily about how we use our money will certainly have expected it to feature largely in this chapter. In fact there is a very good reason why I did not lead off with it. Not that it is unimportant – far from it. But there are dangers in making it the Number One issue:

- People might think that giving their money excuses them from bothering too much about being sacrificial in other ways. Those without much money may say, 'I can't be sacrificial anyway', and consequently not think about the other issues explored in this chapter.

- Those with plenty of money may think that if they give generously they have 'done their bit', so they too do not have to be sacrificial in other ways in church life. They may even (perhaps unconsciously) think their bigger contribution to funds entitles them to a bigger say in church matters. Again, that is

- Scripture consistently teaches that gifts offered to God from disobedient lives are not acceptable to him. This means that other things matter intensely in relation to the giving of our money – the true spirituality of our personal worship, our attitude to others' interests, our readiness to accept change for the gospel's sake, the holiness of our relationships. If these things are not right, our money gifts are not an 'acceptable sacrifice' to God – even though they may be to the Hon Treasurer!

I am not playing down this aspect of sacrifice in our life. Indeed, looking at the Church as a whole, it is depressing how little Christians give. I do believe, though, that if the concept of *sacrificial living* were taken seriously, then *sacrificial giving* would flow naturally from it. Then we should not see nearly so often the familiar prospect of God's work hindered by lack of resources. Christian giving is, ultimately, not about 'supporting the church': it is our response to his love, our share in enabling the work of proclaiming that love. For that reason, I am not going to explore giving even here. It must wait until after we have confronted the call to the whole Church to give itself away to the world rather than concentrate on its own preservation. It is against that understanding of 'God's work' that the whole subject of Christian giving most be considered. Don't worry: the crunch will come!

SIX

CHURCH LIFE – (4) OUTREACH

You are the salt of the earth. But if the salt loses its saltiness, how can it be made salty again? It is no longer good for anything, except to be thrown out and trampled by men.

(Matt 5:13)

It may take a crucified church to bring a crucified Christ before the eyes of the world.
(William E Orchard)[1]

In the local park, our son bounced excitedly in his pushchair and, pointing to a passer-by, loudly asked the standard two-year-old's question, 'What's that?'. 'A man' we replied, slightly embarrassed. Then came the supplementary, disconcertingly direct, 'What's it for?'. Some questions are so fundamental that we rarely, if ever, ask them! Here is another: *'What is the Church for?'* What does the life of your own local church, or indeed the Church at large, suggest it is for?

Matthew's Gospel ends with the 'Great Commission', which we might regard as the Founder's 'charter' for his Church:

'All authority in heaven and on earth has been given to me. Therefore go and make disciples of all nations, baptising them in the name of the Father and of the Son and of the Holy Spirit, and teaching them to obey everything I have commanded you. And surely I am with you always, to the very end of the age.'
(Matt 28:18–20)

In terms of our focus in this book, this commits the Church to 'going', 'making disciples' and 'teaching them to obey [become more like] Christ'. If that is the agenda Christ himself set for his Church, it must be its overriding priority. This is very challenging and potentially very costly.

The Priority of Evangelism

I remarked earlier that I do not believe worship is primarily about evangelism. 'That's a relief,' you may have thought, 'so it *is* all right to carry on just going to church, and leave others to worry about evangelism.' I am sorry to spoil it – but no! Although some are specially called and gifted to be evangelists, the Great Commission confronts us all with the need to put evangelism at the top of our agenda.

The purpose of Christ's mission in coming to earth (to 'bring in the kingdom of God') is now the purpose of the Body he left behind. The Church's *raison d'être* is to proclaim Christ's kingdom in word and deed, until that day when 'the kingdom of the world has become the kingdom of our Lord and of his Christ' (Rev 11:15). Christ assures us

Church Life – (4) Outreach

that the Church undertakes the Great Commission with his authority rather than its own, and with the promise of his continual presence.

> Note that Christ's authority and promised presence relate to the appointed task of making disciples. They are not an open cheque guaranteeing blessing and resources for other things, however right and proper in themselves, in which the Church might choose to engage.

William Temple's famous observation that 'the Church is the only institution which exists primarily for the benefit of non-members' affirmed the priority of its evangelistic task. The command to seek others' good above our own (1 Cor 10:24) is challenging enough as the basis of relationships with fellow-Christians. Now it must be seen as applying also to our relationships with people outside the Church.

'Hold on,' you may say, 'isn't this all going over the top?' Just think for a moment. The Bible declares that people are estranged from God by sin. Christ claimed to be the only way for their relationship with God to be restored. He also said their eternal destiny hinges on that relationship. Given all this, how can introducing them to Jesus fail to be an overriding priority? A rhetorical question . . . but let me suggest an answer! The easiest way to let it fail is to be totally preoccupied with what goes on in church, regarding those outside as nothing to do with us. The Decade of Evangelism was launched precisely because this is how a great many churchgoers do think. We are over halfway through the Decade: have you done anything about it yet?

Christ said, 'You are the salt of the earth.' Salt not only flavours; it also preserves. Through the saving message of the gospel the Church is to be the means of preserving the world. Instead, much of the Church today seems intent on preserving itself *from* the world. Christ's call to self-sacrifice included a serious health warning about the effects of that attitude: 'Whoever wants to save his life will lose it, but whoever loses his life for me will find it' (Matt 16:25).

This is true not only for individuals, but also for congregations. We might re-state it thus:

> The church which believes that its life lies in its own heritage, and concentrates exclusively on preserving it, will find it has nothing left; but the church which realises that its life is in Christ, and is prepared to spend everything to make him known to the world, will find itself renewed and enriched.

The facts bear this out.

> Those congregations which pursue self-preservation most avidly are the very ones which are dwindling, while those which have begun to open themselves up to the needs of the world are growing.

This demonstrates the truth of Michael Ramsey's dictum that 'the church that lives to itself will die by itself'. The first disciples must have been tempted to turn inwards in self-preservation. Their preaching soon provoked opposition. Peter said, 'You killed the author of life, but God raised

Church Life – (4) Outreach

him from the dead' – not exactly calculated to endear him to his hearers! After a night cooling off in prison, the disciples were up before the authorities next day to explain themselves. Peter said it again: '. . . Jesus of Nazareth, whom you crucified but whom God raised . . .'. Luke says: 'When they saw the courage of Peter and John . . . they were astonished and they took note that these men had been with Jesus.' Threatened with dire consequences if they preached in Jesus' name any more, what did the disciples do next? Logic would have argued for caution, worshipping their Risen Lord secretly – at least for a time. After all, how would the gospel be served if they got themselves permanently locked away? In fact, they got together, prayed for even greater boldness, received a fresh outpouring of the Holy Spirit . . . and carried on as before! (Acts 3:11–4:31). Soon they were back in prison. Called to account again, they said, 'We must obey God rather than men,' and left the Council after a flogging, 'rejoicing because they had been counted worthy of suffering disgrace for the Name' (Acts 5:17–42). As they moved outwards from Jerusalem, they were increasingly persecuted. Paul's *curriculum vitae* (2 Cor 11:22–33) makes amazing reading.

Thank God those first Christians did not put their own comfort, safety or (in the case of Stephen, who soon became the first Christian martyr) life itself before the imperative to share the news of Christ's sacrificial death and glorious resurrection. Their boldness shames us for our timidity and self-serving. If they had been like most of us, the gospel would probably not have reached us yet! In all honesty we have to admit our self-centredness, individual and collective. Is it not our unwillingness to sacrifice our comfort, or maybe our image, which so often makes us put our own interests before those of people 'without hope and without God in the world' (Eph 2:12)?

A Growing Church

As a result of the disciples' bold witness, the early church grew at an astonishing rate. Today we deplore generally-falling church attendance. We applaud 'church growth' as a Good Thing in principle. But do we (I mean the 'person in the pew') actually want our own church to grow? Are we ready for the cost involved? Let me give a couple of examples.

One might imagine that 'class' was not a real issue in church life. A quick glance at the average congregation suggests otherwise. The 1985 report *Faith in the City* noted that

> . . . the alienation between Church of England and the majority of working-class people must cause us all to be greatly disturbed. Faced with such a situation the Church cannot persist in the way of self-preservation and that 'institutional self-interest' which so often preoccupies it. It has to move from the policies of maintenance to the outward-looking policies of mission.[2]

The problem is not confined to inner cities. In some villages and remote rural areas, a widespread perception that the Church is for the 'toffs' acts as a strong disincentive to 'ordinary people'. I have an uncomfortable suspicion that congregations do not address this issue because most of their members do not want to. The church is comfortable as a socially cohesive group whose outlook, expectations and interests coincide. Any significant shift in the congregation's social make-up would dilute the culture and disrupt the even tenor of church life.

But we do not have to look far to find even greater challenges. What about those who, for one reason or another, are misfits, people whose lifestyle, personality or circumstances mean they live on the very edge of society? Do we ever think about them in the context of our church? Drug addicts, alcoholics, the homeless, ex-prisoners, the mentally-ill 'in the community', deserted children, abused teenagers, victims of unscrupulous landlords . . . 'There aren't really many such people in our society today, are there? And, anyway, aren't they looked after by the welfare state?' When the Bournemouth church where my wife and I previously worked opened its doors to 'the community' in 1989, we quickly discovered that the answers to these two questions are, respectively, 'Yes, there are many such people' and 'No, they are not generally looked after adequately by the state'.[3] There is a massive, even if officially unrecognised, 'underclass' in 1990s Britain. So – what do you do if you find a teenager turned out of home sleeping in the churchyard: tell him he can't stay there? Or if a mentally disturbed person wanders into a service: do you feel profoundly embarrassed and hope she doesn't come near you?

> How much of the comfort and predictability of church life are we ready to sacrifice for those whose life contains little of either?

It was primarily amongst such people that Christ chose to work: his Body today cannot simply opt out. If they are to find him in the Church, an enormous shift will be required in our perception of what the gospel means and in our willingness to get our hands dirty, sometimes literally, in God's work.

Changed Priorities Ahead

When we mention change, our minds always seem to go immediately to worship . . . not surprisingly, since for so many people Sunday services *are* Christianity. Worship certainly is an area where major changes in outlook will be needed. We explored that a little in Chapter Four. But once we start getting serious about putting others first, there will be other areas of change. These may include:

- allocation of our *money* – perhaps the balance between spending on maintenance and outreach needs to be adjusted, or even reversed;

- use of our *buildings* – opening them up for appropriate use by the community as well as the congregation (I once heard the case put against letting a new church hall to outside organisations in case the paintwork got chipped!);

- mobilising and training our *members* – seeing them not simply as people to help with jobs around the building, but as fellow-workers with gifts to be developed and used in evangelising others and 'teaching them to obey . . .';

- relating to other *local churches* – raising our eyes beyond our own parish, dropping ancient prejudices, and actively seeking deeper fellowship in the gospel.

In 1994, amid intense media discussion about the Church of England's finances, some people expressed unwillingness to pay their Quota share towards the costs of the wider Church. Some congregations which felt they could be self-financing talked of opting out of the Church of England and 'doing their own thing'. This prompted a short but compelling letter to *The Times:*

> Sir, Yes, of course Mr —'s church in the lovely Devon village would be better off if it opted out. But is not Christianity all about opting in, and being worse off?

Discipleship without cost is a contradiction in terms.

* * *

The Church in the World

Evangelism is reaching individuals with the gospel and bringing them into membership of Christ's Body. We have seen that the Church's Founder made this its overriding priority. Speaking at the 'mid-term review' of the Decade of Evangelism in Carolina, USA in October 1995, the Archbishop of Canterbury, George Carey, asserted that 'a church which does not engage in evangelism is simply a disobedient church'. I have already suggested that this disobedience arises from a widespread unwillingness to face up to the sacrifice involved in giving priority to evangelism. But there is another aspect to the Church's purpose in the world. It is equally important, and the two must never be divorced. This concerns how society itself is affected by the presence of the Church in its midst – nationally, locally and as individual Christians.

Let me put it slightly provocatively.

> Compared with the effort we put in to protect what we enjoy in the Church from the effects of meeting the world, how hard does the world have to work to protect itself against the Church?

Does it have to cope with constant Christian challenges to its values and assumptions; a neverending series of powerful initiatives to shape it according to Christian principles; a sense of being infiltrated by Christians intent on bringing about change? If not, why not?

I have noticed a curious paradox in many Christians' attitude here. On the one hand we often hear, 'You shouldn't mix Christianity with politics'. This seems to presuppose that God himself (who 'has no hands but our hands') is not concerned with the affairs of this world. On the other hand, in relation to their own individual lives, they like to think of him as *primarily* concerned with this world – their happiness, wellbeing and fulfilment in the here and now. (They probably had difficulty with my insistence in Chapter Two that such an earthbound perspective hinders our understanding of God's dealings with us.) We cannot have it both ways! To suppose that God is concerned with our *own* wellbeing in this life,

Church Life – (4) Outreach

but not with that of *others*, would be the ultimate self-centredness.

The truth is that God is concerned. We see this in the detailed laws regulating life for the Jews, and the prophets' continual challenge to the moral and social sins of their day. We see it, pre-eminently, in God's plan to save the world, not by some remote act of divine power, but by sending his Son to 'take our flesh'. Christ's incarnation, and the characterisation of the Church as his Body, demonstrate that God has always been, and remains, intimately concerned with his world. If we are serious about discipleship (Body membership), we cannot disclaim or ignore our responsibility as agents of his concern in the world.

This will mean involvement, not just in 'good work' such as charities, but in the places where society is shaped – national and local government, trade unions, business organisations, community associations, maybe on occasions in appropriate pressure groups. The trouble is that, like the day the Teddy Bears have their picnic, for the Church and for individual Christians, 'it's safer to stay at home'! As soon as we raise our heads above the parapet in these contexts, and dare to assert that the gospel of Jesus Christ has something to say about them, we are open to all kinds of dangers. And this is where we have to face the cost of

- sacrificing the comfort of a familiar and generally sympathetic 'churchy' environment;

- sacrificing the intellectual luxury of a faith concerned principally with correct belief, where the minutiae of doctrine seem more real than

the agonies of day-to-day decisions affecting our lives and those of others;
- sacrificing the relative safety of our own territory, and risking being met on 'away grounds' at best with apathy, at worst with hostility, and in between with a range of misunderstanding, criticism, derision and even on occasions dirty-tricks.

In the light of this it is easy to see why most of us (including myself) succumb to the temptation to keep our head well down and not draw too much attention to ourselves as Christians in society. Unfortunately, that is not an acceptable response to the call to discipleship. Bonhoeffer is, as usual, uncompromising but true: 'A community of Jesus which seeks to hide itself has ceased to follow him.'[4]

Being 'Christ's Body' in God's World

Those Christians in our own society who have the dedication to go into public life, and the courage to stand for Christian principles and values, often do so at sacrificial cost to themselves – in the ways outlined above, and maybe in career opportunities and earning power. They deserve more prayer support and open encouragement, not just from individuals but from their house-group or whole congregation. Whether or not we agree with their 'party line', they deserve support for their Christian stance.

The history of the last two centuries (and, of course, earlier times) is studded with those who

Church Life – (4) Outreach

have sacrificed fame, fortune, goodwill, freedom and in some cases life itself in order to bring the light of the gospel to bear on their society.

William Wilberforce suffered ridicule, vindictiveness, and even suggestions that he was mad, because he took his campaign against slavery to the very people whose vested interests were dependent upon it.

John and Charles Wesley were eventually forced out of the established church because they would not suppress their vision to break out of the ecclesiastical straitjacket which largely prevented the common people from hearing the gospel.

William Temple, who died in 1945 only two years after becoming Archbishop of Canterbury, was an inveterate campaigner for social justice. His energetic zeal initiated many of the reforms in social, educational and moral welfare which today we take for granted. But he paid the price: by pricking the conscience of the nation, he sacrificed a good deal of popularity (especially amongst politicians!) – and died tragically early through overwork. How we need to recapture his vision and courage, to call for a society where politicians recognise and foster values which transcend self-interest, and business leaders those which go beyond cash flow and profits.

Janani Luwum, Archbishop in Uganda, was murdered in 1977, becoming a Christian martyr in our own time because, determined to bring the light of the gospel to bear on his society, he refused to be silent about the oppression and atrocities of the Idi Amin regime.

Mother Teresa, perhaps the noblest contemporary example of self-sacrifice, attracts universal admiration for her work in relieving the suffering of many thousands of poverty-stricken individuals. But when it comes to challenging the structures which perpetuate such poverty, then even she is vulnerable to misunderstanding. A television documentary in 1994 viciously attacked her motives; she sacrificed the desire to justify herself, emulating her Lord who remained silent before his accusers.

As the writer to the Hebrews said when he too ran out of space in listing the heroes of faith, 'What more shall I say?' The roll of those who have made great sacrifices to bring the impact of the gospel to bear on society is endless. In our own time they have taken the challenge to Communist regimes, dictatorships, drug barons, corrupt enterprises and every kind of oppression and evil. They stand in a long line of those who have recognised that showing compassion to suffering individuals, although important, is not enough. It has always been part of the prophetic task of God's people also to challenge the godless structures in society which institutionalise injustice. Not only the prophets BC, and generations of disciples AD, but Jesus himself (eg in Matt 23:23–24) saw and responded to this need.

* * *

To root this in the contemporary scene, I end with some examples of things which I believe ought to be unremittingly challenged by Christians. These are issues I happen to feel strongly about. They are only examples; you will have others. There is no shortage of causes!

Social Injustice

Jesus said, 'The poor you will always have with you.' Indeed we do. In most Western societies today poverty arises not from an overall shortage of resources, but from unwillingness to share them fairly. It is more than a cliché to say that 'the rich get richer and the poor get poorer'. Why can politicians and other leaders so easily dismiss talk of the hardship and poverty which exist in Britain, and continue to pursue policies which exacerbate it? Is it not because we Christians are not making much impact? *Faith in the City* was a major Christian assault on the causes of inner city deprivation. At the time it caused considerable alarm about the Church's 'interference' in social problems; ten years on it is having a continuing beneficial effect in numerous communities. Elsewhere, local churches and influential Christians are already doing much in Christ's name to relieve individual suffering. But do they need to be bolder in tackling the authorities themselves on the causes of homelessness, street crime or child neglect? It is hard, unremitting work, very costly and often ending in apparent failure. But then, the Cross looked like failure. In a sense it was . . . until Easter Day!

David Watson wrote in 1978, and it is even more relevant now:

> Biblically and in every age God is on the side of the poor. It is not that he loves the poor more than the rich; but God is essentially the God of justice and righteousness . . . The church, therefore, must be active in its concern for justice and equality, demonstrating God's sacrificial love and concern . . . If

> Christian mission towards the poor is to
> have any credibility, the church must first
> be willing to forego the rights, privileges and
> powers so long associated with it . . .[5]

The Church needs to consider carefully and courageously what that might mean in its own life and structures, and individual Christians in their own lifestyle. As I write in 1995, there is deep public unease about major companies recording record profit levels, achieved largely by efficiency measures which have deprived hundreds of thousands of their livelihood. I must beware of making blanket condemnations, but it certainly appears as if the priorities of business leaders are, in descending order of importance, self – shareholders – customers – staff. There is little evidence that the doctrine of 'trickle-down' (that wealth created by successful business benefits the whole of society) is true. And it will not do to dismiss this unease – as some are trying to do – as merely 'the politics of envy'. To ensure that it is seen to be more than that, a strong Christian voice needs to be heard. Christian politicians and businessmen may need to sacrifice their popularity in order to be the conscience of the nation. Are you a shareholder? Here's a challenge: in order to minimise the suffering and deprivation of others, would you be prepared to exercise your influence on company decisions in ways which might leave you personally worse off?

Business Ethics

It goes without saying that businesses exist to make money for bosses and shareholders. Or does it? An alternative view – that they exist to provide products or services, using profit to develop and sustain their activities – is both morally and intellectually sustainable. It needs to be pressed. Who will do that if Christians do not? There are encouraging instances of commercial enterprise where Christian values actually inform policies. Traidcraft, for example, markets in the richer countries products grown and manufactured in the poorer countries. The producers are usually small farmers or co-operatives in Asian, African and Latin American economies which do not have normal access to world markets. They are paid a fair price for their products so that, instead of being further impoverished by exploitation, their communities and families reap the direct benefit of their work. The company's articles include a commitment to 'promoting love and justice in international trade' and a 'partnership for change which puts people before profit'. Strange language to commercial ears! But this is not playing games. Traidcraft is not a charitable institution, but a company with 4000 shareholders investing over £2 million in capital, and subject to all the normal business disciplines. The big difference is that it regards as 'stakeholders' all who are directly affected by its activities – suppliers, employees, registered retailers and voluntary representatives, and customers. Its performance is externally audited, not only by financial, but also by non-financial, social criteria.[6]

Personal Greed
The National Lottery positively encourages the 'something for nothing' mentality – and not just

something, but unimaginable wealth. If you think this unduly cynical, witness the surge in ticket sales when the jackpot is not five or six, but twenty million. Who could possibly need that much? Why not, on those occasions when the jackpot is not won, give it all to charities? Impossible, of course . . . if you did, fewer people would buy tickets next time, because a public who, only a year ago, would have considered a pools win of £250,000 an unbelievable bonanza, has already come to regard a mere million or two with disdain. The speed at which people's greed threshold has been raised is truly appalling. Matters are made even worse by the cloak of 'good works' under which that greed masquerades. Charities – whose other sources of income are already suffering massively – get less than six per cent of Lottery proceeds. If the motive is really to help others, why could not all those millions of pounds which it now turns out are sloshing around spare in the pockets of ordinary, 'hard-up' people be given direct to good causes? This would release resources ten times what they receive from the Lottery. What incredible things could be achieved then!

So how should Christians react? One year after the Lottery began, church leaders have expressed strong concern about its effect on our national life. But how many local Christian leaders have had the boldness to expose by public pronouncement an attitude of utter self-indulgence which is the very opposite of sacrificial, and directly contrary to the teaching of Christ himself about earthly wealth? (Matt 6:19–21). What about members of their own flock participating in this 'harmless little flutter'? Perhaps they should be challenged

Church Life – (4) Outreach

to demonstrate their discipleship by transferring their stake money to God's work with no thought of personal gain. And how many churches are even banking on getting grants from Lottery funds to keep them going?

*   *   *

Once we start to take seriously the call to be God's people in a world which is his, but which largely ignores him, the issues crowd in on one another. They are often complex; there is rarely a single right answer. That is why it is much easier just to go to church on Sundays, and maybe try to play our part in helping individuals in need, but leave society to look after itself. Edmund Burke said, 'The only thing necessary for the triumph of evil is for good men to do nothing.' For 'good men' read 'godly men and women', and you are very close to the truth!

> To opt out of our share of responsibility for the way things are is to fail to meet the challenge of 'taking up our cross'.

This chapter has only skated over the surface of what it means to be the Body of Christ in the world. But my prayer is that what I have been able to say here will initiate further thought – in particular prompting individuals and congregations to ask themselves some questions. What impact are we making in our area? Is the gospel changing individual lives? Is it being used actively to confront the social issues which need its life-giving insights? If not, is this because we have not thought about it? Or because we do not care about those outside the church? Or because we have given it some thought, glimpsed the likely sacrificial cost – in time, effort, resources and openness to change – and drawn back?

SEVEN

CHURCH LIFE – (5) LEADERSHIP

Be shepherds of God's flock that is under your care, . . . not lording it over those entrusted to you, but being examples to the flock.
(1 Pet 5:2–3)

If the Church as a whole has failed, the ministry has failed even more signally, to exhibit the character of the Servant.
(Michael Green)[1]

Someone once said to me, 'It must be nice being in charge of the music . . . you can choose all your own favourite songs'. That is quite a common view of authority. People think the church leader can do just what he or she likes. But then, how many church leaders give the impression that they think so, too?

This is not the place for a treatise on leadership. We all know that there are various leadership styles; and one is not necessarily more valid than another. But one thing is, or should be, common to them all. In some way or other, they must embody the principle of self-sacrifice. This is difficult, if only because

- most Christian leaders feel they must be seen to be 'strong';
- many church members see self-sacrifice as a sign of 'weakness'.

In terms of everyday (i.e., worldly) ideas of strength and weakness, both are utterly wrong. Of course, in a right sense leaders do need to be strong – in faith, in their grasp of God's word and (as we shall see) in leading their people by example. But that strength will not issue in brutal dominance, arrogance or self-confidence: it is strength 'in the Lord', whose strength is made perfect in our weakness. Conversely, a leader who is constantly giving in to strong-minded members exhibits weakness: avoiding conflict, seeking a quiet life, may be anything but self-sacrificial.

I believe this is a key, if largely unrecognised, issue on the agenda of many churches. So I shall try to tackle it briefly here, although I feel particularly unqualified to do so. What follows is more a series of starting points for further thought than a developed argument.

The Call to Leadership

There are various reasons why people seek positions of leadership and authority. In the world at large, these can be seen to include the desire for power over others, the status of being at the 'top of the pile', and the financial rewards and other perks that go with it. I do not want to be open to a charge of cynicism; so let me say that, in addition, some potential leaders do genuinely believe

Church Life – (5) Leadership

they know in what direction their organisation, company, or maybe the country as a whole, ought to go; they seek top positions in order to be able to move things in that direction. None of these is a valid motive for seeking authority or leadership in God's Church. When I say 'none' I include the last: one of the biggest dangers to a church can be the leader who 'knows what is needed'. I refer, of course, not to the bases of church life clearly revealed in Scripture (exaltation of Christ, love, prayer, faithful biblical teaching and reception of the sacraments, a concern for evangelism – and self-sacrifice). It is always right to lead people in these directions. The danger comes from 'strong' leaders setting additional and specific directions or priorities perceived through their own applied reasoning, rather than through earnest seeking (with others) after the will of God. Commenting on Christ's precise instructions in sending out his disciples (Matt 10:5–6), Bonhoeffer writes:

> All the activity of the disciples is subject to the clear precept of their Lord. They are not left free to choose their own methods or adopt their own conception of their task . . . They are absolutely dependent on the will of Jesus. Happy are they whose duty is fixed by such a precept, and who are therefore free from the tyranny of their own ideas and calculations.[2]

This applies not just to overall leadership in the local church (parish priest, vicar, minister, pastor or whoever), but also to positions of subordinate leadership such as churchwardens, house-group leaders, church secretary and so on. All these need to sacrifice any notion of 'doing their own thing', and devote themselves entirely to seeking, and leading others into, God's will for their fellowship.

The Qualifications for Leadership

The New Testament contains pointers to the kind of people fit to be leaders in the Church. 1 Timothy 3 sets out the qualifications for 'overseers and deacons'. We need not get bogged down here in debate about how these offices may approximate to those in today's churches. The significant — and surprising — point to notice is that there is little about them being people of special ability. Overseers must be

- mature Christians (v 6);
- able to teach others (v 2); and
- well-respected inside and outside the church (v 7).

Even deacons (generally thought to be concerned primarily with the more practical aspects of pastoring) must be strong in their faith (v 9). But, apart from these 'positive' qualities, suitability for leadership is defined mostly by things they must be seen to have renounced. These include an undisciplined home and family life, aggressiveness, a liking for argument, love of money, excessive drinking, short-temperedness, insincerity, dishonesty. Put another way, they must have shown themselves willing to sacrifice all kinds of self-indulgence and self-seeking for the good of the congregation they are called to serve.

The Nature of Leadership

I say 'called to *serve*' quite deliberately. If there is one thing that is crystal clear from the New Testament it is that ministry (= leadership) is above all a matter of service. We noted earlier how Jesus washed his disciples' feet precisely to give them a powerful and lasting picture of what ministry meant. 'I have set you an example that you should do as I have done for you' (John 13:15). From that time on, all truly Christ-like ministry is in the nature of servanthood.

> Michael Baughen, Bishop of Chester, tells how he always keeps a small piece of towelling in his cassock pocket as a constant reminder, amidst all the pomp and ceremony, that his role as a leader in God's Church is to be a servant.

The visual and other trappings of leadership in the mainstream churches today tend to obscure, rather than clarify, its servant nature. Michael Green wrote of vicars behaving 'like a little tin god', bishops happy to be called 'My Lord', and the whole gamut of titles which tend to make the senior cleric 'just a little further removed than he was before from the role of Servant'.[3] They denote power and prestige, whereas the early Christians seem deliberately to have used names which denoted the opposite. *Diakonos* (one who renders service, like a waiter) is used of the ministry of Jesus, the Holy Spirit, Paul and Timothy. *Doulos* (one with no independent status, a slave of others) is similarly used, including of Jesus 'taking the form of a servant' (Phil 2:7).

But even those in Christ's immediate team misunderstood (or forgot) their essentially servant role. James and John asked for the top jobs in Christ's kingdom. The other disciples were indignant – not, I suspect, because it was a wrong request, but because they resented their friends trying to steal a march on them! Jesus had to spell out that in his kingdom the approach to leadership, as to everything else, was the opposite of the world's way:

> 'You know that the rulers of the Gentiles lord it over them, and their high officials exercise authority over them. Not so with you. Instead, whoever wants to become great among you must be your servant, and whoever wants to be first must be your slave – just as the Son of Man did not come to be served, but to serve, and to give his life as a ransom for many.'
>
> (Matt 20:25–28)

To achieve his end by the exercise of his power had been the essence of Christ's own temptations. Had he fallen, it would have compromised his ability to redeem mankind, which could be achieved only through his acceptance of total powerlessness. The desire for power over others – which may be a hidden motive for leadership in the church – spells disaster, quite simply because it *is* so un-Christlike.

The Practice of Leadership

A succinct and challenging snapshot of how leadership ought to work comes in 1 Peter:

> To the elders among you, I appeal as a fellow-elder, a witness of Christ's sufferings and one who also will share in the glory to be revealed: Be shepherds of God's flock that is under your care, serving as overseers – not because you must, but because you are willing, as God wants you to be; not greedy for money, but eager to serve; not lording it over those entrusted to you, but being examples to the flock.
>
> (1 Pet 5:1–3)

There are several important things to note here:

(1) The context Peter sets is the believer's share in Christ's suffering and glory. We noted in Chapter Two how it is only in this sacrificial context that we can understand God's call to discipleship aright. Clearly this applies specially to leaders.

(2) The 'shepherd' metaphor which he uses is rich in associations. In Scripture the shepherd's chief functions are to seek the lost, to lead, feed and water the flock, and defend them against attack. The most notable shepherd of all, Jesus the Good Shepherd, 'lays down his life for the sheep' (John 10:11). The pattern implied by the shepherd metaphor is, essentially, one of self-sacrifice.

(3) The leader must be a willing slave. There are few sadder sights than Christian leaders who have lost any sense of vocation they may have had, and visibly find their ministry a burden or a bore. Furthermore, leadership roles must not be

accepted for personal gain. Although Peter refers to money, there are other aspects of personal gain which might be false motivators – not least that of being popular. What a temptation it is for a minister to build up a personal following: often it is not apparent how far this has happened until he moves on and the life of that church appears to fall apart.

(4) Peter refers to 'God's flock that is under your care' and 'those entrusted to you'. As leaders we often talk about '*my* church', '*my* house group', '*my* Sunday school class' . . . 'there are twenty-four boys and a waiting list for *my* choir'. Granted it may only be a turn of phrase; but it can denote an unconsciously proprietorial attitude towards the church, or group, for which we are responsible.

(5) Lastly, and most important, the main way in which leaders are to lead is by example. In his letters Paul several times tells Christians to imitate him. I used to think this was arrogant. But in one place he elaborates: 'Follow my example, *as I follow the example of Christ*' (1 Cor 11.1; my italics). That is different, of course. And Paul is well able to back it up with evidence: he draws attention to the immense hardship and deprivations he has himself suffered for the sake of the gospel. Read the catalogue of his share in Christ's sufferings (2 Cor 6:3–10; 11:23–27) and you will have to agree that it is some example! Not only that, he also reminds them that he had been prepared to forego the 'rights' that he did have as a leader – like a living wage and a family life (1 Cor 9:1–18) – in order not to be a burden on them. There is even more. This proud Jew, Roman freeman, great scholar and strong leader was prepared to subjugate all this – to become like

a Gentile, under the law and weak – in order to use 'all possible means to save some' (1 Cor 9:19–23).

The Ultimate Purpose of Leadership

If you are a leader of any kind in your church, I wonder how you would answer the question 'What do you see as your ultimate responsibility for those under your care?'. Turning to Paul again, we find: 'We proclaim him [Christ], admonishing and teaching everyone with all wisdom, so that we may present everyone perfect in Christ. To this end I labour, struggling with all his energy, which so powerfully works in me' (Col 1:28).

What an ambition – totally selfless and totally single-minded. Totally unattainable, too, you may think. He admits that it is a struggle (do we expect ministry to be easy?); but he is also aware of the energy of Christ working powerfully within him. The energy that burst the grave ought to be enough for us! And it is worth nothing that Paul expresses this high aim for his leadership in the context of the 'mystery of Christ', which he defines as 'Christ in you, the hope of glory'. This reinforces yet again, as I suggested in Chapter Two, that the struggle can only be single-mindedly pursued, and the sacrifice willingly accepted, in the context of a conscious expectation of sharing Christ's glory. Only then can we give ourselves to the task of leadership in such a way that we work sacrificially, with the needs of those under our care always paramount.

* * *

Can we weave anything useful from these loose threads? In seeking to put the ideals into practice, so much depends on the particular people, places and circumstances in which a leader may be called to serve. Every sphere of ministry has a unique and unrepeatable set of needs. Generalisations are less than helpful. There are, nevertheless one or two broad propositions I dare to make.

First, the leader's primary task is to make and nurture disciples for Christ. It is on their faithfulness in doing this that leaders will ultimately be judged. Until recently I worked with a godly man who is a dynamic leader (the combination is possible!). He has a 'low' view of ordained ministry – liking to describe himself as a 'layman in holy orders' – but a very high view nevertheless of his calling as a pastor and teacher. He reminds his people from time to time – particularly when his actions might be misjudged – that he must ultimately answer to God for the way he has led them. I am always amazed by Moses' action in Exodus 32. The Israelites made the golden calf, and Aaron has just given what must be the most feeble excuse of all time: 'They gave me the gold, I threw it into the fire, and out came this calf'! Moses goes before the Lord and prays 'Now, please forgive their sin – but if not, then blot me out of the book you have written.' His total concern is for the people, however wayward, to be spared to reach the promised land. What a pattern for leadership. I believe that, amid all the many distractions which church leaders have to contend with, it would be very helpful always to remember the ultimate aim of their ministry (to 'present everyone perfect in Christ'), and that it is their faithfulness to this which will be judged.

Secondly, if making and nurturing disciples is

Church Life – (5) Leadership

the essence of the task, then a priority must be to instil in their flock an awareness and acceptance of Christ's call to be 'crucified with him' and live in positive expectation of sharing his glory. This will not be what many want to hear; and even if it is faithfully taught, they will not 'hear' it at all in any meaningful sense unless they also *see* it in practice in their leader's own life and ministry. I have sometimes been disturbed by hearing clergy (or their wives) laying down the conditions on which they will consider moving to a new sphere of ministry – 'nice' area, modern house and so on. As I write, several candidates have declined appointment to one of the Church of England's most senior bishoprics. An 'insider' is reported as saying 'clergy are often happy where they are . . . their wives often have good jobs . . . neither really wants to up sticks and head off for _____'. He added, 'Many people no longer feel it is an enormous privilege to be offered these jobs. To be Bishop of London, for instance . . . is considered a crown of thorns.'[4] A 'privileged' ministry might be grasped at, yes; but one risking painful sacrifice would be shunned. I wonder if the spokesman realised he was virtually quoting Philippians 2:6–8 in reverse! I must emphasise that these are not the leaders' own statements. But the source is said to be an informed insider; and if the picture it paints were only partly true, what a sorry example to every Christian. What more compelling evidence could one imagine of Christians being 'conformed' to the world's self-centred mentality rather than 'transformed' by the Spirit into Christ's sacrificial image (Rom 12:2)?

In this respect above all others, then, leaders both national and local must be an 'example to the flock'. Any idea that the joy of leadership is being able to 'do what you like' must go out of the window. Hard on its heels must go the idea that individuals or groups within the congregation can do what *they* like, or get their own way because of who they are or what they contribute.

> Leaders must be on the watch for any self-centredness in the attitudes and actions of their congregation or group, point it out gently and disallow it firmly.

It is especially important to attend to this where there is a risk that such attitudes or actions may damage the 'weaker brethren' — often those new to the faith or uncertain of it.

Thirdly, even within the Christian community, there is always the danger of sacrificial actions being widely misunderstood. The story of the woman anointing Jesus' feet with costly ointment is instructive. John identifies Judas Iscariot as the source of the criticism of her; Luke attributes it to his Pharisee host, Matthew to the disciples and Mark to 'some of those present'. These divergences, far from discrediting the story, render it utterly believable. It is typical that she was almost universally misunderstood. Only Jesus perceived the truly sacrificial (and, in the strict sense, prophetic) nature of her action.

Fourthly, arising out of this, gaining and keeping popularity must have a low place on the leader's personal agenda. In constantly setting before members the need for self-sacrifice in their church life, and in demonstrating it in his/her own life, the leader will not make everyone happy. Some of the decisions necessary to pursue the

Church Life – (5) Leadership

sacrificial ideal in the fellowship, to protect the weak and to promote the positive change which flows from encountering Christ, will seem perverse to some members. There is a paradox here. The minister who receives constant acclaim and keeps the congregation contented over many years is likely to be regarded as 'successful'. Yet he may at the end have only spiritual 'fat-cats' to present to God, rather than those who by accepting the call to sacrificial living have become more Christ-like. At the bar where it truly matters, his work may be seen to have been weak and ineffectual, and he may be judged to have failed as a leader in this respect. Amidst all the hard demands St Paul made on his young churches – often about overcoming self-centredness – he was always aware of the danger that he might himself fall short of the mark, so that 'after I have preached to others, I myself will not be disqualified for the prize' (1 Cor 9:27).

* * *

I think that, as leaders, we often have an 'image' which we try to live up to – the way we secretly want people to see us. It may or may not be a realistic self-image. More than likely it contains at least some ingredients drawn from the way the world thinks. Preaching about leadership Donald Coggan, then Archbishop of Canterbury, said 'There can be no place for personal vanity or personal disappointment . . .'.[5] We may have to be prepared to sacrifice the image we have, and strive more consciously to make Christ our icon – Christ who, in his humanity, allowed himself to be ignored, rejected, taunted, misjudged, and finally put to death. It is in seeking to imitate that example, and to hold it up to our flock, that we shall be true Christian leaders. The need for such leadership is urgent. As Donald Coggan says:

> The enemy is here – rampant and ready to devour – the enemy that makes . . . a man put his rights before his duties . . . that makes us invert the divine order and put self first, others next and God last . . . that puts the acquisition of things before the building of a Christ-like character.
>
> We need men and women of moral courage, unafraid to stand alone, and willing to say: 'I believe and therefore I will speak'.
>
> We need men and women of self-discipline who know what it is to pray to God:
>
> > Make me a captive, Lord, and then I shall be free,
> > Force me to render up my sword, and I shall conqueror be'
>
> We need men and women of unselfishness, ready to 'give and not to count the cost, to fight and not to heed the wounds'.
>
> We need men and women of vision who have caught a glimpse of what is right, seen the power of a God-guided life, and are prepared to venture and to dare in his service for his world.[6]

EIGHT

MARRIAGE – MADE IN HEAVEN

'For this reason a man will leave his father and mother and be united to his wife, and the two will become one flesh.' This is a profound mystery – but I am talking about Christ and the church.

(Eph 5:31–32)

Marriage is a matter of give-and-take – you give and I'll take.

(Old music-hall joke)

When people say 'marriages are made in heaven' they may mean almost anything – or nothing much at all! But it is on the firm foundation of Scripture that I assert in my chapter heading that *marriage* is made in heaven. Paul declares it to be a representation of the relationship between Christ and his Church. No relationship could be more 'heaven-made' than that; and no other human relationship attracts such a staggering statement. This alone shows that marriage is uniquely significant and sacrosanct. Bonhoeffer calls it 'a parable of the self-sacrificing love of Christ for his Church'.[1] Whether or not our theological stance regards it doctrinally as 'a Sacrament', marriage is certainly sacramental in that Paul is here clearly teaching that it is an 'outward and visible sign' of something far deeper. It is to this deeper 'sacramental' level that I shall seek to look in this chapter.

Marriage is a 'creation ordinance' (Gen 2:24). As such, it applies to everyone. But by making it a representation of the love between Christ and his Church (Eph 5:22–33), the New Testament raises it to a new, sublime level, which can be appreciated only by those who know for themselves the wonder of Christ's sacrificial love. Whenever I use the term 'Christian marriage', it is to marriage on this level that I am referring. It is vital that Christians today should think through the issues of what makes a marriage truly 'Christian'. I say this because:

- of all human relationships, *marriage* has the greatest potential for self-sacrifice, and therefore offers the opportunity for the greatest fulfilment and happiness; and

- of all areas of human life, *sex* is where the world's values are most spectacularly contrary to God's intention, and consequently provides the greatest scope for misery.

Biblical Principles

In this chapter we shall consider three basic scriptural principles. Each has a direct bearing on self-sacrifice, and lays the foundation for showing how the sacrificial principle underlines every aspect of marriage.

(1) Complete Unity

God intends that husband and wife should become a complete unity. This is inherent in

- the original creation ordinance: '... a man will ... be united to his wife, and they will become one flesh' (Gen 2:24), cited by Paul in Eph 5:31;
- the union between Christ and the believer: 'you are in me, and I am in you' (John 14:20);
- the unity within the Godhead: 'I and the Father are one' (John 10:30).

(2) Total Commitment

The New Testament, and Jesus himself, clearly envisage that the pattern for marriage which represents God's intention is a mutual commitment unlimited in scope or duration. The parallel drawn with the union between Christ and his Church leaves no room for a lesser understanding.

(3) Headship

Against the background of the mutual love and care in the relationship between Christ and the Church, Paul develops the principle of the husband's 'headship' in a way which underlines its essentially sacrificial and loving nature.

Complete Unity

We shall look at three areas in which the principle of unity needs to be worked out in practice.[2] The first is essentially the most mundane, but it is also vital. It concerns the day-to-day routine of 'being married', in the almost unending range of patterns and circumstances which occur in modern life.

Give and Take

It is a commonplace that (*pace* the old music-hall joke at the head of this chapter) marriage is a matter of give-and-take. In practice, the exact pattern, personalities and needs of every marriage are different. We should beware (married leaders please note!) of looking at other people's marriages and judging them by our own. An enormous variety of circumstances determine how things actually pan out — work patterns, health, mobility, children, responsibilities for extended family, involvement in church and community life. But taking all these, and others, into account, a regime of give-and-take needs to apply over a whole range of practical issues. These include the household chores and caring for any children or other dependants there may be in the household. Agreement needs to be reached on time spent in the home or outside, and the balance of home responsibilities with each partner's leisure interests. And, of course, there is the matter which (it is said) is the second-largest cause of marital breakdown — money. I believe it would be true to say that, in most balanced and happy marriages, a basic understanding of give and take in such areas has been lovingly sorted out. This makes it no 'big deal' as each particular issue arises.

This kind of understanding is not always going to result in a precise, carefully-calculated, 'fair' balance. Different amounts of 'work' and 'play' may, for example, be possible or appropriate for each partner at different stages in family life. I have yet to meet the husband who can take his turn at breast-feeding! In any event, I refer to understandings being 'lovingly' sorted out, because I am not envisaging a kind of negotiation, with each partner staking out their own interests and together reaching some sort of compromise, in the way a business deal might be reached. One hopes that in any marriage the ingredient of love makes a difference to the way the pudding is stirred. But in a Christian marriage, especially, one looks to see the outworking of the sacrificial principle which underlies it. This involves:

- the general discipleship principle of not seeking our own good, but the good of others (1 Cor 10:24);

- the relationship principle of submitting to one another out of reverence for Christ (Eph 5:21); and

- the marriage principle of imitating Christ in 'giving ourself up for the one we love' (Eph 5:25).

> In short, 'give-and-take' in a Christian marriage should mean each of the partners being more concerned with what they can give than with what they can take.

I found a challenge in a little book published sixty years ago, addressing students about sacrifice. The author points out that even love and friendship can be partly selfish. The thrill or satisfaction

of our loved one's nearness and affection can be
so great that we are at times more concerned
with our own enjoyment of them than with
their welfare. That is possessive rather than
sacrificial.[3]

A glance at something like *The Times*' 'Saturday Rendezvous' column supports this. Men
want someone younger than themselves, attractive, slim, fit, interesting – to make them feel
younger and build up their image. Women assure
prospective partners that they *are* attractive, slim,
fit and interesting, and want a man slightly older
than themselves who is caring, fit and fun to
be with. Nobody wants anyone who will need
looking after, or who will require them to make
allowances or modify their own aspirations –
involve, in fact, any sacrifice of comfort, image
or prospects. Whether they are seeking marriage
or just 'a relationship' (blessed euphemism!), the
governing principle at the outset would seem to
be not 'give-and-take', but 'take-and-take'.

Sacrificial Sexuality
Practical give-and-take issues such as these may
arise not just in marriage, but in friendships
and many other kinds of relationship. But the
sexual relationship is – or rather is intended to
be – unique to marriage. Referring to the 'profound mystery' (marriage representing the relationship between Christ and his people) Paul
quotes the phrase from Genesis 2, 'the two will
become one flesh'. Marriage is sacrosanct because
it represents Christ's self-giving love; but it is
the expression of sexual union ('one flesh') within
marriage which sets it apart. This is important

in our context, because the realm of sex contains both the greatest scope for happiness through true self-giving and the greatest potential for misery through self-centredness. Moreover, this is where the world's attitudes are so pervasive and overpowering that it is almost impossible not to conform to them.

There can be no doubt that we are a sex-obsessed society. (So too, incidentally, were the Greek and Roman societies Paul mostly addressed in his letters.) In common parlance love means sex. And if you want to know what sex means, listen to any pop song on the subject (and most are!) and you will conclude that sex is about getting: what I want to do to you, and want you to do to me – or would do if only you hadn't run away and done it with someone else. (Is this why I react so strongly to worship songs which begin 'I wanna . . .'?!) Other aspects of popular culture share the same outlook; and the vast pornographic industry exists by, and reinforces, the philosophy that sex is entirely about the fulfilment of selfish desires.

Before I am dismissed as a joyless, reactionary old fogey who is 'past it', I had better (like an MP) declare a personal interest. My wife and I thank God that the sexual expression of our love has always been mutually enjoyable and fulfilling. So I do not address this subject as a nostalgic or envious spectator! Like St Paul (when he, too, 'spoke as a fool') I say this not to boast, but to establish credentials. Indeed, if my remarks on this subject seem completely strange to Christian readers, I dare to suggest that this may demonstrate not how out of touch I am, but how far the world's values have infiltrated the way 1990s Christians think about sex.

We have already seen how Christ's call to discipleship imports a major element of self-denial into all our relationships, and how this contradicts the predominant culture of self-fulfilment. Small wonder, then, that the world has largely rejected the ideal of 'Christian' marriage, which exceeds all other relationships in essential selflessness.

> If marriage is a representation of the relationship of love between Christ and his Church, it cannot involve less than total self-giving of one to the other.

It is of that love — selflessly given and freely returned — that marriage is a picture. For sex to be an expression of such selfless love, it must obviously be about more than self-gratification. 'Obviously' to the Christian, that is; for those who do not know God in Christ, the rationale is quite different — if we are just bodies, the 'best we can do ... is to provide them with subjectively pleasurable sensations'.[4] I am not for one moment suggesting that sexual desire and fulfilment have no part; nor that we should not receive, and enjoy, intense pleasure from it. Personally I have no doubt that this is one of God's greatest gifts to us in our humanity. But the greater the gift, the greater the potential for it to be perverted. Precisely because sex is such a powerful and important part of many people's lives, it is where self-gratification most easily dominates.

Sexual acts are intended to be the cement which binds a marriage together, the sacramental sign of constant self-giving in every dimension of married life. The wedding service in the Church of

England's *Alternative Service Book* puts it simply and beautifully: '... that with delight and tenderness they may know each other in love, and, through the joy of their bodily union, may strengthen the union of their hearts and lives.'

This is not meant to make it all sound terribly solemn. One of the great joys which married lovers discover over the years (which I suspect is often missed by advocates of short-term relationships) is that sexual acts between those secure in mutual, self-giving love can vary from the intensely serious, through the lighthearted to the downright hilarious. When the common thread running through them all is that each partner is more intent on what they are giving than on what they are getting, then sex is raised from lust to love. It is then that it truly expresses the total self-giving to which marriage partners commit themselves. And since it is that self-giving which mirrors the love of Christ for the Church, it is then (and only then) that sex becomes 'sacramental' — raised to a sublime level and significance by what it represents.

But do not imagine for one moment that these exalted considerations make sex itself joyless. Far from it: they do not take anything away, but add an extra dimension which enhances it. And it is this kind of 'sacrificial sexuality' which continues to get more enjoyable, significant and cementing throughout a long marriage. By contrast, when partnerships based on a 'selfish sexuality' lose their freshness, there is little left: relationships go downhill, couples staying unwillingly together for economic or family reasons, or maybe separating in disillusionment or seeking new excitement elsewhere. The tragic irony is that millions see the go-getting approach to sex as the way to real enjoyment, and the Christian approach as kill-joy and fuddy-duddy. That is why I asserted that sex is the area of life where the world's values are most at odds with God's intentions – where, in other words, the Devil has a field day in perverting one of God's greatest gifts and deceiving humanity into believing that black is white and bad is good.

It may be objected that I have painted an impossibly rosy, or unattainable, picture. So before moving on to the third aspect of unity, let me just make three brief points.

(1) There are very few couples indeed whose sex life does not have some difficult patches. But where they have learnt during the good times that true fulfilment comes from each putting their partner's needs, wishes and feelings first, they will be more likely not only to survive the difficult times, but emerge from them stronger and more united.

(2) I have clearly been envisaging partners who share a similar level of Christian commitment. I appreciate that the situation will be different where this is not so. There the more deeply committed partner may have to face up to the need for costly sacrifice, regarding the other as (in this context) the 'weaker member', in whose interests their own freedom may need to be curtailed. (See Chapter Three and 1 Cor 10:23–11:1; Rom 14:13–15:4.) Christians with a marriage partner who does not share their faith at all have a great need for understanding and sensitive support from Christian friends. Whether their situation has come about through their own choice, or because they have become Christians since getting married, the result may well be that they and their partner view sex on two quite different levels.

This may call for constant, very costly sacrifice on the part of the Christian partner. To such I can only offer the assurance that God understands; he sees what others do not, and faithful sacrificial living in these circumstances *will* reap its reward, though whether here or hereafter only he in his love and wisdom knows. But let those contemplating future marriage to someone who is not a Christian ponder the command not to 'be yoked together with unbelievers' (2 Cor 6:14) and think through the kind of issues raised in this chapter.

(3) Sacrificial sexuality is an ideal to be aimed at. In this, as in the other areas of life considered in this book, we all frequently fall short of the ideal of total selflessness. When we do so, we are not helped – least of all in our sexual life – by feelings of guilt. We need rather to seek God's grace daily to respond to Christ's call to follow him along the road of self-denial, availing ourselves of his offer of continual cleansing and renewal.

The Married Couple in the Church

Books on Christian marriage rightly emphasise the spiritual level of the union. I want to draw attention to one aspect of this that may easily be overlooked. A good marriage does not come ready made to a couple just because they share their faith. They have to make the same major adjustments as any other couple. Indeed, they may be greater, since the Christian couple are less likely to have been living together already, and more likely to appreciate the enormous commitment involved. Our previous church had an understanding that couples should not bear any major or time-consuming responsibility in church life during the first year of marriage. This is wise. They need to devote time to getting to know one another in a deeper way and adjusting to the change in their identities and priorities.

But there is the other side of the coin. It is possible for newly-married couples to become so wrapped up in one another, so mutually self-sufficient, that they feel no need for the friendship of others or the fellowship of the wider church family. This can easily develop into a settled way of life. This is bad both for them and their church. Having embarked on the mutual self-sacrifice of marriage, they now need jointly to hear the call to live sacrificially. Because of what they find in each other, they may not need others in the same way they did when they were single: but there are others who need them. They should be aware of this, and consider it prayerfully. Teenagers, for example, have a strong affinity with young marrieds, and can unconsciously learn a great deal from sharing in their friendship and home.

Just as a new him/her unit is created as the two become 'one flesh', so the shared prayer, work and witness of a married couple is itself a new creation, something which did not exist before. Each continues to have and exercise their own individual gifts and ministries; but a new spiritual entity, greater than the sum of the parts, comes into being. Bonhoeffer asserts that, as a Christian marriage is 'sanctified in the service of the Body of Christ and in the discipline of prayer and self-control', it will 'even be itself a part of the Body of Christ, a Church in miniature'.[5] Along similar lines Archbishop Donald Coggan said in a sermon about 'proclamation':

> A highly effective form of proclamation is the witness of a husband and wife who share together and pray together. Sometimes this will be spoken proclamation, but often it will not.... As they pray and share together, each partner will find his or her own gifts enriched. Their witness will be more than doubly effective, for in the divine arithmetic, one plus one makes more than two! Such joint witness is a form of proclamation whose effectiveness can scarcely be over-estimated.[6]

I can think of a number of marriages which demonstrate the truth of this. It is a force which could greatly enrich the life, and improve the witness, of many churches. Perhaps it is something many of us have never really thought about. If you are a newly-married couple, think and pray together over this. See what it might mean for you. And if you are not newly-married, it is not too late to catch a glimpse of a new dimension . . .

Total Commitment

God has shown his utter commitment to us by sending his only Son to die for us. The sight of Christ hanging on the cross can leave us in no doubt about his total commitment in self-giving love. And, as we have seen throughout this book, a similar self-giving love is the response required — and willingly given — from those who do see him there by faith. They know what it means to be crucified with him, given a share in his risen life, and filled with his Spirit to live his way, the sacrificial way.

This, too, is spelt out in Ephesians 5 where Paul likens the love of husband and wife to the love of Christ and the Church. The essential point of the parallel is surely this: that the mutual commitment of marriage partners is to be similarly total. This is reflected in the vows to love and to cherish

> for better, for worse,
> for richer, for poorer
> in sickness and in health . . .
> till death do us part.

The commitment thus promised is total in two ways. It is lifelong – not 'for as long as things go well'; and, equally important, it does not depend on circumstances – not 'provided you keep your health, attractiveness or earning power'. It is not even limited by mutual consent – not 'until we both feel we've got all we can out of it'. The commitment of marriage is prior to, and extends beyond, all such considerations.

And, of course, it is not dependent on 'feelings'. A few years ago, a young Christian contemplating marriage to the girl he loved asked us anxiously, 'But how can I know how it will feel to wake up and find her beside me in thirty years' time?'. The question was a good one, because it showed he was taking seriously the lifelong nature of the commitment. The best answer we could give was that you cannot know now how it will feel then; feelings change with both time and circumstances;

Marriage – Made in Heaven

but if you commit yourselves throughout those years to learning total self-giving one to the other, then however it feels, it will be *good!*

We shall consider in a moment why this Christian ideal of marriage is so little understood or valued today. Suffice to say here that for one person to commit themselves so totally and unconditionally to another is diametrically opposed to the predominant culture, where the bottom line is to assert the individual's right to do what seems best for him or herself.

I cannot here deal with the whole question of divorce. But I should not want to seem to ignore the real difficulties that can occur after marriage, or to make light of the agony often involved. Such things can hit Christian marriages, and I feel nothing but loving concern and sympathy for those who find themselves in this situation. What I am seeking to establish is the principle that marriage, as God has given it, involves the *intention* of total commitment. Some people choose to live together without marrying precisely because they do understand this, and are not prepared to make such a commitment. There is at least an honesty about that which deserves recognition. What I find much harder is people embarking on marriage on the basis of convenience rather than commitment – 'if it doesn't work out we can always get a divorce'. Not only is this dishonest (in terms of their vows), but it actually *encourages* them to give up the moment any difficulties loom. I believe that, amongst couples who separate early on in a marriage, there is a good proportion who could have found deeper and more lasting happiness by staying together and working through their problems. Why didn't they? Because prevailing attitudes led them to start without any real degree of commitment to one another.

> I have just read of a couple (American and very wealthy!) whose London wedding plans are coming unstuck because they cannot agree on the financial details of a divorce settlement to be included in a pre-marriage contract.

Total commitment to another person involves sacrificing the notion of the all-important individual whose rights override everything else. Such costly commitment is an essentially Christian concept. Christians, please don't settle for less than this *God-given* pattern of marriage. Like every other application of the sacrificial principle we have considered, it may at first appear impossibly demanding, but in fact it brings unlimited rewards.

Headship

I am walking into a minefield here! However, I should not be faithful to Ephesians 5, on which this chapter is largely based, nor to Scripture as a whole, by avoiding this issue on the ground that it is controversial. Perhaps I may defuse it in two ways. First, let us note what the Bible actually says; secondly, we should see how the essentially sacrificial nature of the headship involved removes from it all overtones which render the very idea objectionable to some.

Marriage – Made in Heaven

In Ephesians 5:21 Paul has enunciated a general principle – 'submitting to one another out of reverence for Christ'. We might describe this as establishing a *symmetry* in relationships, in which those on each side hold the other in the same respect and love. For Christians this principle of 'mutual reverence' is to undergird, and indeed shape, all relationships, of whatever kind. But Paul then goes on to apply it in a number of different contexts – husbands and wives (5:22–33), parents and children (6:1–4), and slaves and masters (6:5–9). Its application clearly varies with the differing circumstances of each relationship: but in each of those quoted there is a built-in *asymmetry*. Parents, for example, obviously have a greater responsibility of care (material and spiritual), and children a greater responsibility to obey and honour – though note how that can and does change as the years go by. Similarly with masters and slaves (a less relevant example today): masters must treat their slaves fairly and kindly, while slaves' primary duty is to give willing, obedient service to their master. In both examples there is a symmetry (all owe one another equal honour and love), but also an inherent asymmetry arising from their respective roles.

Paul applies this similarly to husbands and wives. Christ lovingly and continuously tends and cares for his people (v 29) and is concerned for their wholeness (v 27). Equating the husband with Christ (the Head of the Church), this passage identifies the sacrificial loving, giving and caring role as the husband's. Equating the wife with the Church (which exists and prospers only through Christ's sacrificial loving, giving and caring) Paul identifies her role as one of submission.

Christ 'loved us and gave himself up for us' (v 25). In return he demands our love and total surrender. The symmetry and asymmetry here are obvious. The quality of love given and received is the same; but the roles are different. Human marriage, says Paul, reflects this. The onus on the husband to imitate Christ's total self-surrender is certainly not less demanding than that on the wife to 'submit' to such an amazing love. But I have never heard husbands complaining about the incredibly demanding nature of their role. Why not? Is it because it is not understood — or not taken seriously? Yet the wife's role (portrayed here as a picture of the Church receiving Christ's love) is often rejected today. Why? I have yet to meet a Christian who feels it is in some way unfair or demeaning to be asked to respond in submissive love to Christ's costly offering of himself. Probably this role too is widely misunderstood.

Much of the misunderstanding arises from the quite erroneous supposition that *domination* as distinct from *dominion* (equals headship), and *subservience* as distinct from *submission*, derive from this passage of Scripture. No one can doubt that such a misinterpretation has led to vast and unjust inequalities in the pattern of many marriages in the past. It is all the more sad that the negative characteristics (domination/subservience) have often been seen most markedly among Christians. I have no doubt whatsoever that fresh insights in this area have brought a new quality of mutual respect and happiness to countless Christian marriages today.

In saying this, though, I have to make one important proviso.

> Ultimately, marriages can only be enriched by fresh insights if they are viewed and practised in the context of scriptural revelation and not as a replacement for it.

As we observed at the start of this chapter, marriage is the highest of all human relationships precisely because it 'sacramentally' represents the love between Christ, the Lord of Glory, and his people, the Church Universal. Human life offers no higher privilege than the call to live this out between two people. We cannot afford to trifle with the revelation thus given.

This brings us to a matter we must consider briefly, not only in relation to headship, but to all that has been explored about marriage in this chapter. It is the climate in which we have to try to maintain and live out this most exalted of relationships.

Contemporary Culture

We have already noted how Christians are liable to be affected by the prevailing outlook of their generation. The outlook of the last decade or so could be summed up as (i) the pursuit of self-fulfilment and (ii) the assertion of individual rights. An important contributory factor – perhaps the main one – in this has been feminism. Its concern with relationships between men and women has spread out and shaped the way society views all relationships. With deeply-embedded gender injustices throughout society – no less in the

Church than elsewhere – corrective action was certainly long overdue. But concern for the status of women developed a social outlook where the assertion of 'rights' has coloured the very way people think and live. Similarly, concern to open up channels for women to fulfil themselves has bred a philosophy in which individual 'self-fulfilment' for all is the prime goal. Despite the obvious gains in all this, the net result of constantly asserting 'rights' and avidly pursuing 'self-fulfilment' has been to produce a society which is increasingly self-centred.

> We are all now largely conditioned by a mind-set in which the notion of self-sacrificing commitment one to another is not seen as a valid, let alone ennobling, pattern for human relationships.

This culture is the exact opposite to that of the gospel, where Christ calls all who would follow him to 'deny themselves, take up their cross daily, and follow him'. This faces the Church with a subtle temptation – to present a gospel in which Christ's sacrificial call is 'spiritualised', diluted or omitted altogether – a gospel which, by reflecting the spirit of the age, can be portrayed as more 'relevant' and therefore better. Where the Church falls into that temptation it fails both its own members and society. (See Gal 1:6–10; 1 Cor 2:2; Rom 12:2.)

There is no doubt that men's domination and abuse of women has been widespread and regarded as acceptable – including (in some instances, one is ashamed to say, especially) among Christians. Underlying attitudes certainly needed to change, and in some ways still do, if only to bring our behaviour up to the minimum requirements of the gospel in which 'there is neither ... male nor female' but all are 'one in Christ Jesus' (Gal 3:28).[7] (If you are anxious about my use of this text, please read the note.) In these circumstances, the fact that the resurgence of feminism (it is *not* new!) has at times been destructive and bitter is hardly surprising – though it is regrettable. But such attitudes have never been the sum total of feminism; happily in the mid-1990s a less strident ethos seems to have emerged.

I have gone into this because it has been the main factor shaping society's view – and hence influencing the way today's Christians think – of marriage. We must learn to take what is good from it. But it is vital that we should recognise the underlying values and priorities for what they are. For all the reasons we have seen, 'rights' and 'self-fulfilment' – essentially self-centred, assertive attitudes – have no place in Christian marriage. Marriage is, as we saw, truly 'Christian' when it strives to represent the total self-surrender of Christ, without which there would be no salvation, no faith, no hope – and, ultimately, no love for any of us.

Christian Singleness

Before leaving the subject of marriage, I should add a word about, and to, those who are single; because, although many are entirely secure in their single state, others do feel let down – not least by their church. The Bible encourages us to regard singleness, just as much as marriage, as a gift from God (see 1 Cor 7). But I use the heading '*Christian* singleness' very deliberately. Just as I have suggested that a marriage, to be truly 'Christian', must reflect the self-giving love of Christ, so I believe that truly Christian singleness displays essentially sacrificial characteristics.

Some have consciously let the opportunity for marriage go by, maybe in order to fulfil a specific task or calling, such as lifelong missionary work overseas. Others have responded to family responsibilities, such as the care of parents, only to find that the freedom and opportunity to marry passed them by. This is undoubtedly a vocation for some: like all vocations, it is costly, and worthy of respect. Sadly, such people are sometimes treated within a church fellowship as nonentities, or neglected altogether. Years of devotion to their vocation may mean that, by the time they surface as people in their own right, they have less sparkle and a narrower circle of acquaintances than others. And, of course, they are less inclined to talk endlessly about babies, schooling and careers! People whose lives revolve around such things may find them less fun to be with: but their experiences will have taught them valuable lessons which others have missed. So one way for those who are married to show respect is to listen carefully to them, and value what they say. This will bring mutual benefit. And we should take every opportunity of offering singles love and friendship; consciously including rather than excluding them; showing that we recognise the difficulties of facing the future, and possible old age, without the love and support of a marriage partner. In doing so we shall not only be affirming them, but also playing our part in building up the Body, which (see Chapter Five) is the responsibility of every member.

Finally, a word to single people themselves. 'Sacrificial' singleness implies that there can be the opposite. It is just as possible to be selfishly single as selfishly married! Singleness, *per se*, is not necessarily sacrificial. Not everyone is single as a result of a costly decision. Others of us are single because we have found nobody to marry us, or out of personal choice. Such singleness need not be self-centred. It may be turned to good account. We might consider how we can best serve our church by our relative freedom from the ties of marriage and the family. Can we offer our gifts or skills (as musician, accountant, teacher, gardener, car driver . . .) rather than letting a married person with young children struggle to keep up with work, family and church responsibilities? Alternatively, can we offer to babysit (not always waiting to be asked first!) so that parents can continue to use their gifts in the church – or just get out to worship together? By such actions – and others like them – we too would be playing an important part in building up the Body.

* * *

There is much more I should like to have written. In the realm of marriage and sex, millions see self-centredness as the norm, and self-restraint as irrelevant or old-fashioned. These attitudes have infiltrated Christian circles so subtly that, thinking we have moved with the times, we may not recognise them for what they are. I am deeply convinced that, as fewer and fewer people are even aware of Christian (as distinct from merely traditional or 'British') standards, it is by being truly Christian in our relationships that we can make the most important, and far-reaching, contribution. As singles, marriage partners, or (as we shall now go on to consider) parents, homebuilders and citizens, the distinctive Christian-ness of our lives will be that they are essentially sacrificial. It is time to fight back against the world's self-centredness – and our only weapon is the Cross. The call to us all is to:

> Be imitators of God, therefore, as dearly loved children and live a life of love, just as Christ loved us and gave himself up for us as a fragrant offering and sacrifice to God.
> (Eph 5:1–2)

NINE

FAMILY LIFE – TRAINING IN DISCIPLESHIP

Then God said, 'Let us make man in our image, in our likeness . . .'
(Gen 1:26)

Let no debt remain outstanding, except the continuing debt to love one another . . . Love does no harm to its neighbour. Therefore love is the fulfilment of the law.
(Rom 13:8, 10)

What we see is a world which has rejected love, because love required the glad giving up of self to another. Human beings choose to be ignorant of this rejected love, and to inhabit a world constructed by their own selfish desires.
(Keith Ward)[1]

The Bible tells us that the Son 'by [whom] all things were created' (Col 1:16) and the Spirit of God 'hovering over the waters' (Gen 1:2) were active with the Father in the creation of the world. This unique Trinitarian God incorporates personal relationships within his own being, yet remains one God. An unfathomable mystery, maybe: but it is fundamental. The twin facts that

- relationships are at the heart of the life of God himself, and
- we are made in his image,

have immense implications. Two of the most significant are that (i) being a Christian is, essentially, experiencing a relationship with God; and (ii) Christian discipleship is lived out at a practical level primarily in terms of relationships.

In approaching the whole matter of relationships, of whatever kind, this must be our starting point. Sin shattered the image of God in all mankind. Christians are those in whom it is being restored. It follows that we should expect to find that image stamped on our relationships: they should reflect the relationships within the life of the Godhead. There is mystery here beyond our understanding; but it is apparent that the essence of the relationship between the Father and the Son is mutual self-giving love. 'For God so loved the world that he gave his one and only Son . . .' (John 3:16); Jesus, 'being in very nature God, did not consider equality with God something to be grasped, but made himself nothing . . . and became obedient to death' (Phil 2:6–8). Mutual self-giving love is, then, the pattern for all Christian relationships.

> ### A SURPRISING PRINCIPLE
> Because Jesus' relationship with his Father was perfected in his sacrificial obedience, and we are made in God's image, this means that our relationships are more nearly perfect the more sacrificial they become.

This is a complete reversal of the world's values, which tend to regard good relationships as those

Family Life – Training in Discipleship

which give you what you want. From this root of selfishness have grown a variety of aggressively assertive attitudes to others, which have become regarded first as acceptable and then as admirable.

I know that 'family' does not mean only father, mother and 2.4 children! A married couple with no children are an embryonic family; and most of us know of extended families which include a grandparent, in-laws, lodgers, foster-children and so on. Some Christians today choose to live in small communities. I do not want anyone to feel left out (as some are said to do by Family Services). Having said this, I hope I may be forgiven for directing this chapter mainly towards the family where children are being brought up. There is an urgent, even desperate, need to re-establish Christian values to challenge the prevailing self-centred individualism and 'rights' mentality. This need can best be met by encouraging Christian parents to re-examine their own values, and assisting them to raise a family where mutual self-giving love is understood and accepted. By focussing on this I do not mean to exclude other Christian households, or to be insensitive to those who are childless. Above all, I recognise that there are some who, in answering a particular call from God, may have voluntarily renounced the opportunity of having children. This itself may represent immense sacrifice on their part.

Nor, in using 'parents' throughout this chapter to mean a married couple with children, am I insensitive to single parents. The death of a husband or wife, mutual separation after marriage breakdown, or (sadly) one partner walking out on the other, can happen to Christians. Some have become Christians since such events in their life. Then there are those seeking to establish a Christian family life, but whose partner does not share their faith. I hope that readers, whatever their circumstances, will find something of value here as they seek to give children a Christian upbringing. I ought to add, though, that I do firmly believe that the best way to bring up a family is with the continuing and committed presence of both a father and mother. Christians should regard this as the norm, to be departed from voluntarily only in the most exceptional circumstances. I realise that saying this contradicts the current ideology which asserts a woman's 'right' to have children for her own fulfilment – outside the mutual care and responsibilities of marriage if she so chooses. That represents the kind of rampant individualism and self-centredness which, as we saw in the previous chapter, can all-too-easily be accepted by the Christian community in its desire to be seen as relevant and contemporary. The fact that it concerns 'women's rights' must not be allowed to cloud the issue. Any behaviour which emphasises only the supposed 'rights' of an individual (of whichever gender), showing little or no recognition of responsibilities towards anyone else, is a denial of the sacrificial principle. For this reason alone, such attitudes have no legitimate place in Christian discipleship.

Back to Basics

'It is not good for the man to be alone' (Gen 2:18). Human beings are made with an inbuilt longing for friendship and love. Granted this is stronger in some people than others; but the individual who *never* feels the need to relate to others is very much an exception. (In practice, it usually transpires that such rare people, through being damaged in some way, suppress rather than lack the instinctive desire for relationship.) Adam and Eve, the embryonic 'family', were made to be mutual friends, helpers and lovers; to enjoy together the worship of God and the care of his creation; and to share in his creative work by being pro-creators. It is interesting (but idle!) to speculate how their family life might have developed had they not fallen into temptation. Their sin, which was the entry of self-centredness into human existence, shattered their relationship not only with God, but also with one another. Recrimination soon broke out; and their relationship of mutual delight becomes one of domination and pain (Gen 3:16). Most poignant of all, in just one generation the intended blessing of family life turns into painful sorrow. They watch horrified as their firstborn, Cain, in his self-centred desire for acceptance, murders his own brother.

Thereafter the Old Testament is full of family heartbreak – rape, incest, jealousy, trickery, betrayal . . . all of 'tabloid' human life is there. Almost without exception, the cause of the unhappiness and mayhem is self-interest. But there are also noble examples of sacrifice in family life. Abraham shows himself willing to sacrifice Isaac, the only child of his old age, on whom all God's promises depend (Gen 22:1–19). Hannah, childless for years, gives her son Samuel back to the Lord as a temple servant, not even keeping him at home long enough to enjoy watching him grow up (1 Sam 1:21–28; 2:11).

Here, then, is a first principle of Christian family life. 'Lo, children and the fruit of the womb are an heritage and gift that cometh from the Lord' says the psalmist (Ps 127:4 Book of Common Prayer version). To see our children as gifts from God is to recognise that, like everything else he gives us, they are first and foremost *his*, and only secondarily *ours*.

Starting a Family

'A dog is not just for Christmas,' warns the RSPCA. Is it really necessary to point out that a similar principle applies to children? Evidence suggests that it is. Self-centredness in parenthood can arise from the very start. True we are given maternal and paternal instincts so that (at a biological level) the species survives, and so that (at a theological level) we may experience the fulfilment that comes from sharing God's creativity in this particular way. Of course a baby can bring immense happiness and fulfilment to its parents; however, it does not exist primarily for their benefit, but they for its. Realising this may avoid much misery. Let me mention two common, but potentially unhappy, reasons for starting a family.

(1) *Having a baby to fulfil a parent's own emotional needs*. Those who had an unhappy childhood may seek to make up for this in some way by having a baby of their own. No doubt they are convinced that they will be able to give their child the happy upbringing they missed. Sadly, statistics show that it is more common for the pattern of unhappiness to be repeated. A child brought into

being mainly to repair emotional damage in one or both of its parents, or to try and keep together an ailing marriage, is very vulnerable. At best it will receive 'need love' rather than 'giving love'. At worst it may be rejected when it fails to fulfil the purpose its parents intended. Of course, this may not always be the case. The grace of God can and does transform lives. But Christian parents in this situation need to think and pray earnestly about their reasons for starting a family.

(2) *Starting a family because you like babies.* This is all very well – but babies have an incurable habit of growing up! Liking bonny babies is not enough: what about capricious children, aggravating adolescents and tiresome teenagers? They are not all as bad as that, of course – but I'm sure you see the point. In entrusting to us the ability to reproduce, God has given us a very precious thing. With a baby comes long-term responsibility for the physical and emotional care of another person, made (like us) in God's image. Even that is not all: this new person has a soul – immortal, yet brought into the world by an act of our own will. Parents bear the awesome responsibility for the spiritual nurture of that soul. Paradoxically, they must also recognise that this new independent person they have brought into being has its own free will, and must ultimately make its own choice to exercise saving faith or not.

This is all serious stuff – not the kind of thing you think of when you make a baby! It may sound totally overwhelming. But Christian parenthood is actually meant to be fun! How can this be? Because, as with everything God asks us to undertake, he gives us the gifts to do it.

And there is great joy and blessing in doing it: but *only* if we do it his way – the sacrificial way. There are few places where the paradox of self-sacrifice can more clearly be experienced than here.

> Having children solely for our own pleasure or self-fulfilment is liable to turn sour and bring neither. Conversely, while devoting ourselves totally and sacrificially to the interests of our children may seem a tough demand, in practice it most often brings deep joy and lasting fulfilment.

Setting an Example

Young children take in more than we think. If they are to grow up seeing the Christian life as sacrificial, they must observe it in their parents. We have just seen how marriage itself is potentially the most fruitful ground for growing self-giving love. Children will learn more from seeing this between their parents than from any other source. But it should be reinforced by an explicitly sacrificial element in the way parents treat their children. I am not encouraging parents to be doormats for their children's increasingly large feet. Quite the reverse. I believe that, once children are old enough to begin to understand – maybe in the early school years – they should be positively taught to exercise self-restraint towards others. The point is that they can only be expected to do that if this is the atmosphere in which they have grown from babyhood.

Family Life – Training in Discipleship

I am not suggesting that we should make this a 'big-deal' in family life. Parents need not go round like a kind of Uriah Heep saying at every turn 'Look, Johnny, isn't Mummy being sacrificial?'. It should all be very natural and unselfconscious. It is about relationships which, because they are based on mutual submission 'out of reverence for Christ', are open in recognising and responding to one another's strengths, weaknesses and needs. A home in which this is the prevailing atmosphere will be a natural cradle for children who are aware of others as well as themselves, and who learn instinctively to value and respect other people and property. Then the Christian attitude of 'looking to the interests of others' can be instilled without the hypocrisy of asking of them something which the parents themselves do not practise.

> Our local TV news carried the story of a child in a village school who was so allergic to bananas that even touching the skin made him very ill. All the other children decided, with their parents, never to take bananas to school. I found this simple example of sacrificial concern very moving.

But children can only learn from their parents if they spend 'quality' time with them. This raises questions which will be contentious, where in recent years the agenda has largely been set by issues of self-fulfilment and the assertion of individual rights. I can only draw attention again to the fact that Christ's call to sacrificial living demands an outlook totally different from those who 'inhabit a world constructed by their own selfish desires'.[2]

Parenting – Top Priority

Those bringing up children today face very different challenges than their own parents did. There have been vast changes in economic climate and social attitudes. For many families in 1990s Britain, life is a constant battle to make ends meet and provide the children with the minimum necessary for their welfare and education. Enormous pressures can arise within families trying to live partly or wholly on State benefits. And when work is available for one or both parents, there are decisions to be made which may involve agonising choices. Single parents often face special difficulties here. Those of us who are older, or better off, should perhaps show greater understanding and sympathy than we sometimes do to those bringing up families against the odds.

But parents with better earning opportunities also face pressures. The constant quest for a higher standard of living can dictate the pattern of working and family life. Once *things* take priority, enough is rarely perceived as enough. Parents can imperceptibly slip into a lifestyle which means devoting more time and energy to earning, and less to their young children, than is desirable. Christian parents, in particular, need to be constantly aware of the dangers of accepting the world's values uncritically. Doing so may deprive their children of the upbringing they need, in an atmosphere not only of stability but also of mutual self-giving love. Moreover, parents' own values here are inevitably projected onto their children.

That is to state the potential problem. But what is the answer? There is no single answer. Patterns of employment and society have changed so rapidly that the traditional family template of the bread-winning father and the home-making mother no longer applies. There is no reason to regard that as necessarily a bad thing. Where both parents have the skills and opportunity to work, they must talk and pray about what they should do. All kinds of factors may affect their decisions – their respective earning potential, long-term career prospects, the nature of their work, any special needs of their particular family. And the combination of circumstances will change. Decisions may arise whether to move (for career advancement) or to stay (maybe for a child's educational stability). During the years when there are young children in the family, priorities will need to be kept constantly under prayerful review by both parents together.

My purpose in raising this is not to attempt to suggest an answer – but to put up a marker for Christian parents to recognise the importance of giving priority at this stage in their lives to the high calling and responsibility of the care and upbringing of children. Working this out will almost certainly – indeed should – involve some sacrificial cost. It may affect immediate finances and lifestyle. For those in professional or high-flying careers it may involve lowered, or at least deferred, career expectations. It may mean, for a time at least, foregoing altogether the fulfilment of going out to work. Any such decisions Christian parents make in these matters may be perceived as foolish by non-Christian friends and colleagues; they may have to be prepared for implied criticism, or even amused scorn. Pray God they may receive more understanding from their Christian friends.

Of course, priorities which intrude into family life may not be connected with earning, but with pursuing self-fulfilment through a hobby, or possibly study. They may even arise from church membership. This raises the spectre of becoming too busy 'being Christians' to give priority to being parents. Bonhoeffer points out that the obstacles which stand in the way of obedience to Christ's call may often themselves present a very respectable face – such as 'responsibility and piety'.[3] A brother and sister wrote to the Church Mission Society's postal Bible-school with some questions. 'We can't ask our parents,' they explained, 'they're too busy being missionaries.' How sad. Commitment to the life of our church is a fine, and very necessary thing. But while there are young children in the family it may be right for parents to review their contribution to church life – particularly where it takes them out of the home. This is especially important where one or both has a demanding full-time job – which they must also aim to do well to God's glory. Reviewing commitments in this way should not be seen as a cop-out. For some, indeed, giving up church work which they find creative and deeply fulfilling entails considerable self-sacrifice.

The other side of the coin is equally important. Church leaders and other members should be ready to sacrifice their freedom to call on such people's talents, at least for a while. This should be done not grudgingly, or with suspicion, but in full affirmation of the parents' recognition of a period during which raising a family is the right priority.

Of course, it is not really a case of family *or* church. As soon as children are old enough, it is highly desirable for service in the church to become part of family life. This may be either by mutually supporting one another's church activities, or by joint acts of service. Such things as families leading intercessions, going out together to deliver church magazines, or taking responsibility as a family for visiting a sick or elderly person, are excellent ways of building up both family life and unselfconscious servant attitudes. Leaders – do think of families *as families*. A church we knew made children sit with their group or organisation at Family Services, not with their families.

Growing Up

At the drop-in centre opened by our last church, many who came in found it hard to cope with life, or had become social misfits in some way. When they began to open up, we heard the same story in nine cases out of ten: their problems as adults stemmed from relationships with parents. Their stories highlighted two particular ways in which parental selfishness occurs as children grow up. Both look like laudable concerns for the children's good, and are therefore not easily recognised for the self-centred attitudes they actually are. This may sound harsh. But since they have been shown to be so damaging, I cannot avoid drawing attention to them here.

Pressure to 'Succeed'
The first concerns parental expectations. It usually starts with education. What parent would not

want their child to do well at school? Interest, encouragement and support are needed at every stage; but it is a fine line between this and putting them under undue pressure. Sometimes parents behave as though intellectual attainment were the only measure of a person's worth. 'Dave has done very well at school . . . but Kevin has never been any good.' How many Kevins have grown up with that ringing in their ears? Even to think, let alone speak, like that is to deny the very basis of Christian faith about what gives a person worth. A strong assertion, you may think. That is because I could introduce you to a dozen people whose lives have been clouded — some virtually destroyed — by a deep-rooted sense of failure to live up to expectations. No doubt their parents thought they were acting in their children's best interests. So let me suggest some of the motives that actually drive parents in this respect:

- They want their children to demonstrate educational prowess (for example a university degree) which for one reason or another eluded them.

- Being able to recount their children's 'success' is one of the ways in which they compete (consciously or unconsciously) with neighbours or colleagues.

- A family tradition of going to 'good schools' must be maintained, whether or not it suits the individual child. This can be particularly subtle: the financial cost (possibly involving hardship) can make it seem very sacrificial, though the real agenda may include the avoidance of a social stigma.

Family Life – Training in Discipleship

- Their children must get a 'good job' in order to keep up the family's perceived place in society.

Such selfish motives may start early on, and persist into college days and beyond. By then the pattern is set. Parents' continued use of their growing children as a means of expressing their *own* aspirations can have a lasting and harmful effect on the young adults' ability to set their own goals and take responsibility for their own lives.

Failure to Let Go

Ability to let go of our children is a reliable test of parental selflessness. Of course, youngsters develop at different rates; but for all normal children the time comes when their interests would be best served by allowing them to begin learning how to exercise independence. In the matter of friendships, for example, parents should naturally be concerned and offer guidance, especially to teenagers, about conducting (but not avoiding!) friendships with non-Christians. But discouraging, or even trying to veto, friendships with kids who are OK, but just aren't exactly the kind we should choose to have hanging around our house – that may reflect a selfish concern with our own comfort or image. Here again, I do not want to sound judgmental, because the line between healthy parental guidance and domination is a fine one.

The letting-go stage has certainly been reached by the time they go to college, or want to move out to a flat on their own or with friends – or, of course, to get married. These crucial events may serve to highlight for those of us who are parents where 'need love' has played as large a part as 'giving love' in bringing up our children. So long as they remained practically and emotionally dependent on us, we derived satisfaction and self-respect from meeting that need. This is not to question the genuineness of such parental love and care. But, as children grow towards adulthood, they need to be allowed — even encouraged — to break (but oh! so gently) those ties of dependence. It is when parents cannot see this, or seeing it cannot face up to it, that the truth emerges about the time, care and attention they lavished on their family all through the growing years. What may have *appeared*, to them and others, to be very sacrificial, has contained all along a large element of unconscious self-centredness.

Again, I could cite many adults who have been totally unable to break away from the vice-like grip of parents. We remember going to tea with Anne (not her real name), an educated and highly talented musician of around sixty. She was not allowed to pour the tea until her ninety-year old mother gave the word — then came in for severe criticism of the way she cut the cake. Comical? Yes, at the time; but after years of mental instability and depression she took her own life. Then there was Gwen, who dropped out of university at twenty, fearing to fail her parents. Her life went steadily downhill until, having reached the depths, she visited our drop-in centre, found acceptance and friendship, renewed her commitment to God, and began to straighten herself out. Now in her early forties, she wanted to go back to college and regain lost opportunities. The problem? Despite having had very little contact with family for almost twenty years, her mother's expected disapproval of her plans still loomed so large as to seem insurmountable.

These may be startling examples; but on a less dramatic scale they are multiplied countless times. Why do we cling so tightly to our growing children, still wanting them to be dependent 'babies'? Why are we so hurt when a 'child' in their twenties wants to leave home? And obviously it is very nice if we can share our offspring's unlimited enthusiasm for a potential marriage partner; but if there are some things with which we do not immediately 'click', is it right to put pressure on them on this account? All of these are instances of behaviour which suggests we regard our children as existing to fulfil our expectations, even when they become adult. And we should *never* pressurise our married children to start a family because we want to be grandparents!

Letting go *is* hard. It is liable to reveal things that have been suppressed. Parents whose marriage has been deteriorating, suddenly have to face being alone together. A single parent now recognises the fear of utter loneliness, of not being needed any more. The widow, who has been able to see her lost husband so clearly in her growing son, feels his departure almost as a second bereavement. To describe such feelings as self-centred sounds harsh and censorious. I do not want to be either. Perhaps it would be better to say that failure to put children's needs first at this stage in family life shows just how earthbound we are. I think Jesus may have had something like this in mind when he uttered those apparently heartless words (Luke 14:26) about needing to 'hate' our own family in order truly to follow him. It is a relative statement. Love for our families is among God's greatest gifts to us: but they are still to take second place to God himself, whom we are to love with all our heart, soul, mind and strength. Having given us the amazing power of bringing new persons into being, God gives us also the responsibility of doing all we can to lead them to saving faith in Christ. Paradoxically, it is if we succeed in this that they will come to love God above everything – including ourselves. This will seem hard if we are 'earthbound' – that is, able to think of our children only in relation to ourselves. But if we can raise our vision to take in the eternal dimension, we shall be able to see them not just as *our* children, but as *God's* children, 'co-heirs with Christ' (Rom 8:17), all of us striving together to love him above all else. This is not a lower, but a higher, experience of Christian family life. We shall love our children more, not less; but it should help to stop us clinging to them.

I realise that this will not be easy to accept. To some it may even sound heartless. But, as C S Lewis observed, 'it's cruel not to say it.' Natural affection, he says, has something in it 'which will lead it on to eternal love . . . But there's also something in it which makes it easier to stop at the natural level and mistake it for the heavenly.' He adds (it is a person already in heaven speaking):

> But someone must say in general what's been unsaid among you this many a year: that love, as mortals understand the word, isn't enough. Every natural love will rise again and live forever in this country: but none will rise again until it has been buried.[4]

Finally, before leaving this, it is important to balance what I have said, by recognising a very special kind of parents. I am thinking of those

Family Life – Training in Discipleship

who would gladly let go – may indeed have looked forward longingly to the day when they could. Instead they find themselves shouldering family responsibilities even heavier than when their children were young. This may be because of a grown-up son or daughter's long-term illness, perhaps the failure of a marriage, or continuing financial problems. What parents had anticipated as a time of relaxation and relative freedom turns out instead to be one of anxiety and burden-bearing. This can be very hard. I know of one couple who have given up their time and freedom – even sold their home – to try to help with their children's problems. This is immensely sacrificial. At times, when even their own costly efforts to help seem unavailing, they must long to walk away, and leave their children (who are, after all, independent adults) to sort out their own problems. Then it takes more than the bonds of human love: it is only through God's grace that parents in this kind of situation can go on loving and giving, apparently endlessly. When they do so, it is a real sign of the mark of Christ's cross on their lives, a living picture of the sacrificial love which took him through the cross to the glory beyond.

Passing on the Benefits of Sacrifice

It is an observable fact that our family life tends to reflect patterns unconsciously absorbed from our own parents. My experience with people over the years suggests that this is particularly true of parental possessiveness. I think of an old lady who has expected to see her daughter every day since getting married almost thirty years ago. Perhaps it is not surprising then, that the daughter, now in her fifties herself, finds it very difficult to let go of her own grown-up children. What most people would regard as exceptionally possessive parenthood has certainly affected the life of the next generation in that particular family. I do not know how far it may go back. I mention this because it adds a larger dimension to the question of how much giving and taking we do as parents. It means that the level of sacrifice or self-centredness in our own family life may affect not only our children's lives, but those of our grandchildren – and so on. A sobering thought: but it has a positive and happy counterpart, on which I want to dwell for a moment. Where we are conscious of having benefited from sacrificial attitudes on our parents' or grandparents' part, we might make a specific resolve, with God's help, to pass on those benefits to our own children. It is as though we have held them in trust only until such time as we can hand them on.

A real-life example may help. One couple's married life began with the wife's parents, of modest means themselves, generously setting them up in their first home. Thirty years later one of their own children was in similar need. After prayer, God enabled them to see it as an opportunity to hand on, with thanksgiving, the conditions for security and happiness that had flowed to them from their parents' sacrifice. Acting on this, they had the additional reward of their other child fully approving the plan without a hint of 'what about me?'. The concept may be applied in less material ways. If, for example, we know that our childhood was surrounded by the faithful prayers of our parents, could we commit ourselves before

Family Life – Training in Discipleship

God to do no less for our own children? Just think – we can be the means of transmitting to future generations the benefits of sacrifices made by our own parents or grandparents.

Of course, this idea may leave you cold, because you are a 'first-generation' Christian. Or it may leave you burning hot with anger because you cannot look back on your own upbringing with happiness or gratitude. If so, I am sorry. But please do not feel entirely excluded from this. Every 'chain of blessing' of the kind I have outlined started somewhere. With God's help, *you* could be a starting point. Why not aim to make following Christ's sacrificial call such a priority in your family life, that *your* children will grow up blessing you, and showing a desire to pass on the benefits of your sacrificial love to their children?

This whole concept has a biblical ring about it. We cannot read the Old Testament without being struck by the fact that the family was absolutely central to the life of God's chosen people. And central to family life was the idea of passing on from generation to generation the deeds by which God had made and confirmed them as his people.[5] Psalm 78 is a great catalogue of God's mighty works, intended as a means of passing on faith within families. 'Listen,' says the Psalmist, 'I will utter hidden things, things from of old':

> what we have heard and known,
>   what our fathers have told us.
> We will not hide them from their
>   children;
>   we will tell the next generation
> the praiseworthy deeds of the LORD,
>   his power, and the wonders he has done.

> He decreed statutes for Jacob
> and established the law in Israel,
> which he commanded our forefathers
> to teach their children,
> so that the next generation would know them,
> even the children yet to be born,
> and they in turn would tell their children.
> Then they would put their trust in God
> and would not forget his deeds . . .
>
> (Ps 78:3–7)

Observe, then, how family life is another area in which God's intended blessings are spoilt or lost altogether by the self-centred individualism which passes for wisdom today. If only we could set the world's pattern aside, and catch something of that inspiring vision of ourselves as links in a chain of faith and blessing spanning the generations. Then our supposed individual rights and the freedom to major on self-fulfilment, could be renounced, and seen as comparatively small, short-term, sacrifices. The stakes are so much higher than just our own comfort or achievements. The call is so much nobler, the rewards so much greater.

Seizing every opportunity for sacrifice in families is a wonderful way to experience the self-giving love of Christ our Lord. More than that, it draws a simple, unmistakable picture of that love in our own generation, a witness that may convey more than thousands of words . . . and sows the seeds of unseen and untold blessing for our children and our children's children.

TEN
LIFESTYLE AND COMMUNITY

All things come from thee, and of thy own have we given thee.

(1 Chron 29:14 RSV)

But godliness with contentment is great gain ... For the love of money is a root of all kinds of evil.

(1 Tim 6:6, 10)

All life in the kingdom will essentially be life for others; life outside ... is always predictably every man for himself.

(Michael Marshall)[1]

If the idea of passing God's blessings down through families has an Old Testament ring, this is because the centrality of family life to the Jews produced a sense of security and continuity. This remains true today, even where they live in societies which, like our own, have largely neglected or rejected such ideas. In the Old Testament 'family' and 'community' are often used interchangeably. This being so, family life may properly be regarded as a training ground for life in the community. This highlights the importance of our attitudes and priorities within the family. Do they

- reflect the sacrificial attitude which Christ exemplified himself and demands of his followers?
- set a pattern for an unselfish life outside the home – in our church and local community?

In order to understand this chapter, it is important to establish one overriding principle at the outset.

Owners or Stewards?

'What do you have that you did not receive?' (1 Cor 4:7). We are all inclined to regard our possessions, be they few or many, as ours by right. Yet a moment's thought will show that, however we have come by them, we have in a real sense 'received' everything we possess. True, we may have earned them by hard work – hours of overtime maybe! But who gave us the skills, or health and strength, to do it? That's just naive and childish, some might say. Simple, certainly, but not naive; child-like, but not childish. Above all, it is profoundly biblical. However we regard the first chapters of Genesis, they certainly contain absolute truth about the relationship between God, ourselves and the world. God gives mankind everything needed for his wellbeing, with

Lifestyle and Community

responsibility for its care and lordship (dominion) over other created things. The mess in which we find ourselves today arises from exercising the dominion, but denying that it is God who gave it.

The Old Testament, Jesus' teachings and the New Testament letters all say the same: collectively as the human race, and individually as members of it, we are *stewards, not owners*, of everything we have. A simple enough concept — but with profound implications. It means we are not free to do just as we like with what we have. Do we find such a statement disturbing? If so, we need to ask ourselves why. If it seems to threaten our freedom, or limit our ability to enjoy our possessions, is it perhaps a sign that we have never fully realised our need of Christ and received his gift of eternal life? Compared with that great act of faith, which involves humbly admitting our *total* dependence on God's mercy, it is a small thing to acknowledge his supremacy over our material possessions. When we truly appreciate the extent of God's love for us as an individual, it is not hard to recognise that everything we have comes from him and belongs to him. It becomes not a confining concept, but a liberating experience. I would sum it up thus:

> All that we have comes from God; it is held in trust from him and is to be viewed and used accordingly. Any attitude towards possessions which denies this is less than fully Christian.

One factor transforms this from a hard saying to a welcome truth: love — God's love for us and ours for him. In saying this, I immediately scent danger: the picture of God as an indulgent parent giving us what we want. We have already seen (Chapter Two) how preoccupation with health, wealth and happiness is too earthbound a view of our status as God's children and his purposes for us. Some do teach that faithful Christian discipleship guarantees material prosperity. The roots of the Faith Movement (or 'prosperity gospel') go back into the last century. Its general effect is to change our relationship with God from simple trust in his undeserved goodness into a formula for worldly success. Not surprisingly, this has attracted millions of people – particularly in America, where it brings together the natural religiosity and the emphasis on material prosperity which both characterise the 'Great American Dream'. Recently it has taken hold amongst some Christians in Britain and elsewhere.

Obviously I cannot deal with this fully here. But in our context I must make three important points:

God's Purpose for His Children
There *is* a connection between God's love and his material blessings. But it is not one of direct cause and effect. Despite particular Old Testament texts, the Bible's *overall* teaching does not encourage us to see prosperity as the chief sign of God's love, or as a reward for our loving him. It is certainly heretical (and damaging) to teach that those who are *not* well off are falling short in their discipleship. Anyway, regarding the rich as specially favoured is wide of the mark, and covetousness is expressly forbidden. The purpose underlying all God's dealings with his children has to do not with material prosperity, but with growing Christ-likeness.

The Bible's Warnings About Wealth
Christ himself taught that wealth was likely to be a distraction which could disrupt, or even ruin, discipleship (Mark 10:17–30; Matt 6:19–21). The epistles contain similar warnings. Most explicitly, Paul warns the young pastor Timothy that those who 'think godliness is a means to financial gain' are teaching 'false doctrines' contrary to the instructions of the Lord Jesus Christ (1 Tim 6:3–10).

The Cost of Discipleship
In warning of the dangers of setting our hearts on material things, Jesus presented discipleship as involving immense cost (Matt 16:24–26). His promise (Mark 10:28–30) that those who have left all for his sake will receive back many times more 'in this life' is easily misunderstood. It is not some kind of sanctified investment plan! It is fulfilled in the experience of belonging to God's family, where the unsearchable riches of Christ, and the relationships in which we share them, are of a new and deeper kind than anything we might have given up. In any case, we surely cannot believe Jesus was saying 'sacrifice all in order to follow me, then I will give you more earthly goodies with which you need not be sacrificial'. The call to sacrifice has no end in this life. If we do receive material things after we have committed ourselves to Christ in discipleship, they are given to us as new opportunities for sacrificial stewardship. Surely this is what John Keble meant when he wrote

> If on our daily course our mind
> Be set to hallow all we find,
> New treasures still, of countless price,
> God will provide *for sacrifice*. (My italics)[2]

John Wesley (one of the founders of Methodism) earned over £30,000 from his writings in his lifetime, but he left very little when he died. His accounts show why:

	Earned	Spent	Gave Away
Year 1	£30	£28	£2
Year 2	£60	£28	£32
Year 3	£90	£28	£62
Year 4	£120	£28	£92

This is consistent with Christ's teaching that 'from everyone who has been given much, much will be demanded' (Luke 12:48). Finally, it is vital to notice that Christ's promise in Mark 10:30 about rewards for those who give up all to follow him is made in the over-arching context of 'the age to come'. We must always be on our guard against 'cupboard love', which is tempted to follow Jesus for what we can get now.

Warning: Even Good Things May Seriously Damage Your Health!

God gives us so much for our enjoyment – beauty in nature and art and the ability to appreciate it; work to do and skill and strength to do it; scientific discovery and medical knowledge; the security of home and community; above all, the love of friends and family. The list is endless. Nor is it invalidated because many people do not have all these things. Of course we must show compassion to those deprived of health or senses, home, security, family, love or self-worth. If we can, we must direct part of our own sacrificial love in their direction. But the fact that not everybody has an 'easy' life does not call God's goodness into question. (If you feel it does, go back to Chapter Two – better still tackle the book of Job with a good commentary!) The story of the widow putting her tiny coin into the temple treasury (Luke 21:1–4) shows not only that sacrifice *can* be practised by those who do not have much, but also that it *should* be. In praising her, Jesus never hinted that she need not really have gone that far.

So what follows about the dangers of possessions is for every reader – however much or little you may have. It is easy (and understandable) for those with very little to covet more. But the evidence is that even those with plenty still want more. On the very day I write this, two men who have just won over £22 million on the national lottery said they will certainly buy tickets again next week! Conversely, when it comes to giving, it might be expected to be easier for the better-off: but evidence shows that it is often the poor who give more – not only proportionately, but sometimes in real terms.[3]

It is not the amount of our possessions, but our attitude to them, which matters. 'If riches increase, set not your heart upon them' says the psalmist (Ps 62:10 KJV). Perhaps Paul had this in mind when he wrote: 'Command those who are rich in this present world not to . . . put their hope in wealth . . . but to put their hope in God, who richly provides us with everything for our enjoyment' (1 Tim 6:17).

Enjoyment! What is it, I wonder, about us Christians which has given Christianity a reputation as a killjoy religion? Nothing could be more untrue. The New Testament certainly contains many warnings against sinful pleasures: first-century Graeco-Roman society was as decadent as ours. But there is also a discernible 'theology of pleasure'.[4] God *has* 'provided us with everything for our enjoyment'. When we ignore his good gifts, or treat them with suspicion or even disdain, we impoverish ourselves, demean the faith and show ingratitude to the Giver. Strong language, but intended to provide a firm, positive background against which to view the warnings which follow – warnings which are needed to prevent us from setting our hearts on God's gifts, rather than on God himself. Moreover, they guide us towards true fulfilment, leading us to the discovery that the same principle applies to possessions as we have already observed in relation to church life and relationships – that they bring greater, not less, satisfaction when viewed and used sacrificially.

Here, then, is Paul's warning:

> But godliness with contentment is great gain. For we brought nothing into the world, and we can take nothing out of it. But if we have food and clothing, we will be content with that. People who want to get rich fall into temptation and a trap and into many foolish and harmful desires that plunge men into ruin and destruction. For the love of money is a root of all kinds of evil. Some people, eager for money, have wandered from the faith and pierced themselves with many griefs.
> (1 Tim 6:6–10)

And he tells the Corinthians: 'From now on . . . those who buy something [should live] as if it were not theirs to keep; those who use the things of the world, as if not engrossed in them. For this world in its present form is passing away' (1 Cor 7:30–31).

The New Testament perspective on money, possessions and legitimate pleasures might be summed up thus: they are entirely good, given for the Christian's enjoyment, but held in trust from God, and to be regarded lightly as passing things. Bonhoeffer sums it up:

> [Christians] have everything as though they had it not. They do not set their hearts on possessions but are inwardly free. That is why . . . they can leave the world when it becomes an impediment to discipleship . . . [They] use worldly goods . . . with thankfulness and prayer to the Creator of all good things. But all the while they are free.[5]

The Consumer Society

This freedom of the individual spirit is the very opposite of what businessmen and politicians want. Bent on economic growth, they want us all to be enslaved to the notion that we must have the things they produce. To attain their goal of economic prosperity they must create a climate in which our needs (or rather wants) are constantly stimulated, met by their products, then subtly modified in order to be met again. This process keeps the whole merry-go-round of advertising, free samples, special offers and 'new improved' products turning. And what is wrong about that? A great deal.

(1) *It encourages self-centredness.* Sometimes this is quite explicit . . . 'go on, indulge yourself' says the ad. More often it is subtle. But by constant, unremitting action, like water wearing away a stone, the message of consumerism causes us to confuse needs with wants; to put our own wants before others' needs; to become dependent on 'things'; to believe that in order to be 'fulfilled' we must have what we did not know we wanted until they told us! Somehow this message seems more relevant and insistent than Jesus' reminder that 'a man's real life is nothing to do with how much he possesses' (Luke 12:15, Phillips).

(2) *It ignores the consequences.* As well as damaging ourselves, morally and possibly physically, self-indulgent excess is almost always at other people's expense. Nations with economic muscle continue to exploit those without, thereby robbing our fellow men and women now. In order to feed our insatiable appetites, we continue to pollute and over-exploit the earth, thereby robbing future generations of a sustainable environment.

(3) *It violates God's purposes.* Mankind was given the earth with the command to 'work it and take care of it' (Gen 2:15). Freedom was to be exercised with restraint: he could eat of any tree but the one. Freedom with restraint underlay the Old Testament laws – every seventh year a sabbatical for men, animals and the earth; corners of the harvest field left for the poor to glean for themselves; a jubilee once every fifty years in which debts were cancelled. Restraints such as these were designed not to fetter, but to benefit, mankind. Blind to this, we plough on in unrestrained excess towards personal, local and global disaster. Everything from Sunday trading to massive exploitation and

pollution is justified by that overbearing freedom – the freedom to make money.

Is all this an exaggeration? And what has it to do with a sacrificial Christianity anyway? In 1973, Donald Coggan (then Archbishop of Canterbury) saw things just as starkly. He spoke of the insistence that 'we must get the last ounce, or the last inch, out of everything'; and that was before the rise of accountants as the gurus of all business enterprise! Similarly, before the far greater excesses of the last two decades, he said a revolt is needed 'against the prodigality of a society which puts profit before people, and which is prepared to rape and violate nature provided that luxury is promoted'. And, he added, 'who better to initiate and foster it than the Christian disciple?'.[6]

This thought was developed by John V Taylor (former CMS General Secretary and Bishop of Winchester) in his book *Enough is Enough*.[7] Written in 1975, it remains startlingly relevant and challenging. He referred to growth in profits at the expense of jobs; the fallacy that growth in wealthy nations enriches poor nations; ruthless excess which regards any restraint as an affront. Today his claim that our excesses threaten the *quality* of our children's lives appears an under-statement – twenty years on, it might be nearer the mark to say their very lives themselves are at risk. The problems have got no better for being recognised, and the challenge to Christians remains largely un-met.

Of course, there are bright spots. The Church Urban Fund (established by the *Faith in the City* report) has made an impact in some deprived inner city areas. Christian communities in various places aim to live and promote a simple lifestyle.

The Movement for Christian Democracy aims to bring Christian concepts to bear on the political culture.[8] CARE (Christian Action, Research and Education) has been set up to promote Christian values, particularly in family life, through lobbying and practical charitable action.[9] Then there is the occasional inspiring individual example, like a local authority transport director accepting the inconvenience of public transport because he feels unable to drive to work when his job is to urge others not to.[10] But generally I suspect we all feel the problem is just too big. Anything we could do would make no impact; so we do nothing.

The problems of the selfish society *have* to be tackled. Scientists, environmentalists and those economists who can see beyond the end of their nose — now recognise that we cannot go on as we are. Society generally exhibits a kind of schizophrenia. Public figures whose lifestyle is conspicuously self-denying (like Mother Teresa) attract widespread admiration. And, as Ian Bradley observes, a growing recognition that our self-obsession has resulted in high levels of crime and stress-related problems and illnesses has produced an openness to the need for radical, possibly unpalatable, change to put things right. Yet the very fact that the remedies are unpalatable causes people to ignore or reject them. They involve 'being prepared to surrender, let go, limit desires and postpone wants, seeing beyond immediate gratification'. More and more people can see this in the context of the environment. But limiting our greed to ensure our own survival is still only a form of enlightened self-interest. The call which needs to go out to the world goes deeper than this. It goes beyond the level of humanism.

Lifestyle and Community

Self-centredness is a deep spiritual malaise. We must challenge head-on the prevailing wisdom of the age, a wisdom now becoming sharply focussed in New Age teachings and philosophy – which talk endlessly about *self*-fulfilment, *self*-gratification and *self*-realisation. That is the real challenge for Christians today.[11]

Families Show the Way

> A girl was walking along a beach where thousands of starfish had been left stranded by a particularly high tide. Every now and then she stopped, picked one up and threw it back into the sea. 'Why are you doing that?' someone asked, 'there's so many, it can't make any difference.' 'It does to this one,' replied the girl, as she threw another starfish back into the water and watched it come to life.

We *can* make a difference. We must not let the scale of the problem paralyse us into inaction. Because it rests on unlimited sacrifice, the gospel speaks uniquely to our situation. The Christian family (using the term in a broad sense) is the most likely – maybe the only – seed from which a new, less selfish, society might grow. Experience shows that you cannot legislate, top-down, for people to be less self-seeking. But if Christian families enter fully into the life of their local community, there is no telling what influence they may exert. Provided, of course, that their lifestyle *is* distinctively Christian – and that means sacrificial.

John Taylor writes: 'It is not enough to talk ... We need a thoughtful, convinced minority that will *live* in such a way as to challenge the cherished beliefs of the consumer society and defy its compulsions.'[12] He calls for a 'joyful resistance movement' to be established by a 'counter-culture of families and groups that cannot be conned or manipulated because they simply do not accept the accepted values or pursue the ambitions that are expected of them'. He goes on:

> We need a rapidly increasing minority that is entirely counter-suggestible . . . that calls the bluff of the trend-setters, is a dead loss to advertising agencies and poor material for careers advisers . . . Our need is for men and women who are free with the freedom of Christ, free to ask the awkward questions that have occurred to no one else, and free to come up with startling answers that no one else has dared to give.[13]

Too many of us have been taken in by the world's line. We have let ourselves be lulled into accepting that a self-centred approach to daily living is normal and inevitable. Maybe we cannot even see it for what it is. It is time to wake up! 'Do not be *con*formed . . . be *trans*formed . . .' John Taylor suggests three slogans to help families prick the bubble of complacent consumerism:

- The price tag is too high.
- Who are you kidding?
- You can't take it with you.[14]

It is no use a lifestyle based on some such ideas being a grudging compromise. It can only hope to influence the community if it is seen to be a joyful, positive thing. *And it can only be that where Christians have discovered the truly liberating effect of living sacrificially.* We are back to where we began: everything we have is a gift from God, ours to use as stewards not owners.

Sacrificial Christian Family Lifestyle

Bishop Taylor hoped that his ideas might spread outwards to form 'cells of dissent', or be applied in wider groups or congregations. But, taking the family as the basic seed, how might these Christian values be implemented within the home? Because people's circumstances vary so much, I must not be too hard and fast. But here are some pointers which I hope readers may want to think about in their own families. They are important both in themselves and in the sacrificial model they might provide for the community. After all, actions speak louder than words.

Christian Giving

It is vital for all Christians to give financial support to the church's work. Personally, I would regard it as normal for most of our giving to be directed through our own church: if we feel unable to trust the leaders of our own fellowship to use our gifts wisely and faithfully to further God's kingdom, there is a serious problem. But church giving can denote *merely* a response to the local church's needs, where we imagine that the pound coin in the collection plate sufficiently discharges our responsibility to support God's work. Our horizons need to be wider than that . . . hence my heading 'Christian giving'.

> A Christian lifestyle should begin with a deliberate act of setting aside a proportion of our income for direct giving to God's work, and as a conscious symbol that the rest of our possessions are also committed to him.

Some Christians take the Old Testament prescription of a tithe (tenth) as the basis of their giving. Others recognise that, since this was a requirement of the law, true 'freewill offerings' began only beyond one-tenth. Still others assert that we are now 'not under law but under grace', so tithing is irrelevant. This may well be a correct theological stance: but we do well to note that in Christ's 'the law said . . . but I say to you' statements, his requirements went *beyond* those of the law. (See, for example, Matthew 5:21–48.) Of course Christians are free, and should give according to their conscience. Unfortunately – and this is not to be judgmental – the evidence suggests that the giving of a great many Christians is (i) not systematic but spasmodic (when they happen to go to church); and (ii) does not approach anywhere near one-tenth of their income.

The New Testament has a good deal to say about giving. Unlike today (when it is often said that the last part of a person to be converted is their pocket!), the first Christians seem quickly to have realised the implications of their faith for their lifestyle. We know (Acts 2:44–45) that they sold their possessions and gave to those in

Lifestyle and Community

need; for the rich this included major possessions such as houses and land (Acts 4:32–37). Ananias' and Sapphira's attempt to deceive the fellowship about their giving was extremely serious, and led to their death (Acts 5:1–11). But there were poor Christians too. The Macedonians were both poor and persecuted, but Paul speaks of how their 'extreme poverty welled up in rich generosity' (2 Cor 8:1–15). Their giving was truly sacrificial; they 'gave as much as they were able, and even beyond their ability'. This is the kind of giving he holds up as an example to the Corinthians, whose approach seems to have been rather grudging. He exhorts them not to give 'reluctantly or under compulsion', exphasising that 'God loves a cheerful giver' (2 Cor 9:6–7). It is not new for Christians to resent God's intrusion in this area of their lives. What was it about the Macedonians' giving that was so special?

- *It was first and foremost a response to God himself.* 'They gave themselves first to the Lord and then to us . . .' (2 Cor 8:5).

- *It welled up from sincere love.* They 'pleaded . . . for the privilege of sharing in this service to the saints'. Their love for fellow-Christians grew out of their love for Christ who 'though he was rich, yet for your sakes he became poor, so that you through his poverty might become rich' (1 Cor 8:9).

Giving, says Paul, is a 'test of the sincerity of your love'. In my experience, people who truly know themselves loved by God rarely have any problem about giving. Churches which have undertaken major projects or initiatives often attract the comment 'you must have a very rich congregation'. Not necessarily: where the gospel is faithfully and powerfully preached, and God's love is shown amongst the members, their natural and willing response is to show their gratitude and love to God and his people in their giving. That is what happened when the tabernacle was being built; eventually Moses had to order the people to stop giving 'because they were bringing more than enough for doing the work' (Ex 36:2–7). Imagine that today – a congregation giving so much they had to be told to stop!

'We will not offer to the Lord offerings that cost us nothing'.[15] For all of us – poor or rich or somewhere in between – a worthwhile challenge is to ask ourselves whether there is anything we're not able to have or do because of what we have given to God? By definition, sacrificial giving is costly. In a sense, it will 'hurt'. Isn't this just religious masochism. Not at all. Sacrificial giving is an essentially *joyful* experience. How can this be? It is the same paradox – strange yet true – that we have noted in other aspects of this study. The joy lies in:

- *the source of our giving*. Willingness to give sacrificially grows from a deep, personal awareness of God's fatherhood, his own sacrificial love in Christ, and the gift and power of the Holy Spirit.

- *the outcome of our giving*. There is deep satisfaction (not the same as complacency) in obedience to God's will. 'You will be made rich in every way so that you can be generous on every occasion' (2 Cor 9:11). Many can testify to their own spiritual growth as a result of committed giving. Often we may be able to see tangible results, as God's work moves forward and lives are changed. Your giving, says Paul in 2 Corinthians 9:11–15, will result in others thanking God for your obedience and generosity, praising him and being stimulated to prayer.

My wife and I will always be grateful to the couple who first encouraged us to take committed, prayerful, costly giving seriously. If you have not yet done that, let us commend it to you. Be an agent of God's love in your own church, the wider mission in the world, the relief of poverty and suffering, and 'secular' activities designed to cement and improve your own local community. Christian giving is costly: but it brings great joy and blessing, to others and to yourself. And it all flows from the love of God in Christ.

> Thanks be to God for his indescribable gift!
> (2 Cor 9:15)

Simple Living

A telling slogan a few years ago was 'live simply that others might simply live'. We have already seen how global problems demand a less excessive lifestyle from the richer nations. But most of us can only take action at the level of our own family and community. Of course, some reading this book may be living at or near the breadline. Although (as I have already tried gently to point out) that in itself does not exempt them from the call to sacrifice, they are unlikely to be able to answer it by simplifying their lifestyle. But I suspect that for most of us there are priorities which should be reviewed, and questions which should be asked, before God, about our family budget.

- How far have you fallen for the advertisers' ploys? What *is* the overwhelming advantage of a round tea bag? And do you really need to try something because it is 'new' – the same old crunchy snack, but in the shape of a car instead of a dinosaur? Or is this a chance to teach your family something worthwhile about self-restraint which will stick with them as they grow up?

- Is it really justifiable to spend £1500 rather than £500 on a hi-fi, for a 5 per cent difference in sound quality which, for half the time, you won't even notice? If you can really afford that extra £1000, what else might be done with it?

- Do you actually *need* a large, expensive car with a thirsty engine? Or is it to create, or keep up, an image? If you had a much more modest vehicle, and gave the difference in running costs every year to the church, how might this enable God's work in your own community or further afield to be extended?

- Do you participate in the lottery because you have swallowed the line that it is about helping good causes? Ask yourself before God if that is really why you take part? If it is not, re-read Jesus' words in Matthew 6:19–21, and Paul's warning in 1 Timothy 6:6–10. If it is, then why not give your weekly stake money directly (so that they get 100 per cent of it, not just 6 per cent) to, say, a missionary society? There is no better cause than spreading the gospel.

These are, of course, arbitrary examples. We all have our own interests and temptations. Mine is collecting books! Perhaps we regard such things as nothing to do with our faith. If so, we could not be more wrong. James reminds his readers sternly of the link between faith and deeds, and how the first without the second is a contradiction – dead, in fact (Js 2:14–26). And John writes: 'If anyone has material possessions and sees his brother in need but has no pity on him, how can the love of God be in him? Dear children, let us not love with words or tongue but with actions and in truth' (1 John 3:17–18).

Let there be no doubt that charitable relief *is* God's work. The gifts of the Spirit include giving to those in need (Rom 12:8) and practical help (1 Cor 12:28). And we should never forget Christ's solemn warning (Matt 25:31–46) to those who see human distress but fail to accept any responsibility to relieve it. But undoubtedly the 'brother in need' also includes all those, throughout the world, who need the knowledge of Jesus' saving love. There is always a need, starting at our own doorstep, for more resources to proclaim the gospel in word and deed. Consequently there is always for Christians a balance to be struck between that universal need and the legitimate needs of home and family. I am not going to be so foolish as to suggest any generally applicable 'right' answers. But I do urge you to ask yourself the questions. And I do so not only because it enables our own spiritual growth, as adults, to face up to these issues, but more particularly for the good of your children. It is vital to bring up a future generation of Christians less self-centred than we (I mean collectively) have tended to be. So let them *see* restraint at home, both in what you have, and in what you allow them to have. This may involve them in a bit of early exposure to the pain of not having what 'everyone else' at school has. Be with them in that pain. As they get older, *discuss* these questions with them. Help them to understand why a Christian lifestyle needs to be different. When they can, let them contribute to family decisions.

> By learning to enjoy living simply, and passing on that enjoyment to your children, you will be making a contribution of immense consequence to their own future and that of the community.

Just imagine a generation of Christians who have learnt to say 'if we have food and clothing, we will be content with that' (1 Tim 6:8); who have the courage to opt out of the rat race; who have learnt to make 'who are you kidding?' their response to most advertisers' claims;[16] and who generously use the resources they thus save to further God's work in their local church, community and wider world. This is possible, because attitudes, like blessings, are handed down through families. You only have to think how much your own outlook reflects your upbringing to know that. It is very hard to bring up children today – maybe harder than ever before because of the unprecedented extent and power of the media. Parents today have the future largely in their hands: if you do not shape your children's lifestyle, there are others with millions of pounds to invest in doing so. It is in all probability only from your own example that they have any chance of learning a responsible, truly Christian (i.e., sacrificial) lifestyle.

Hospitality

Both Paul (Rom 12:13) and Peter (1 Pet 4:9) urge Christians to offer hospitality gladly. Of all Scripture's exhortations to Christian living, this must be one of the most sadly neglected by Christians in Britain today. We can probably all think of homes where we always feel welcome. Even on a casual call, what a warm feeling that gives us. But this is more than balanced by those where we never get beyond the doorstep. How many fellow church members have invited us to their home in the last year? How many have *we* asked to share a meal – or just a cup of tea or coffee – in our home? This can be guaranteed to deepen relationships within a congregation; and deepened relationships tend to stimulate mutual care and prayer, enliven corporate worship, and thus strengthen a church's witness. Again, as we saw earlier, our individual contribution affects the whole church family. For most of us, offering simple hospitality (I'm not talking about a five-course banquet!) would involve no great effort. And yet so often we do not make the effort. Why?

But, important and neglected though it is, I am not thinking just about offering hospitality to fellow-Christians. What about using our home to meet non-believers? Here, I suspect, some of us who score a few points on the above paragraph, draw back. I confess that I do. Yet there is overwhelming evidence that people who would not dream of coming to church may well open up to conversation about their life, hopes and anxieties in the surroundings of a home. Here, surely, is the first, and best, place for family and community to meet and interact. This is where Christian lifestyle will make an unselfconscious impact on others. This underlines the importance of Christians cultivating in their home and family a simple, unostentatious and relaxed lifestyle. In such an atmosphere the less well-off will not feel threatened, while the well-heeled are unlikely to be put off. Among the most heart-warming experiences my wife and I have shared over the years have been those times when people have said 'I like being in your house . . . it's got a nice atmosphere'. They did not seem to mind the non-matching furniture!

> Never under-estimate people's ability to sense Christ's presence in your home – even those who do not recognise it for what it is. Make sure it is not obscured by your lifestyle.

The Englishman's home is said to be his castle. That often means we go in and pull up the drawbridge after us. Of course, there is a need for our home to be a sanctuary, where we can retreat and just be ourselves, unwind, recharge our batteries. All of that is important. I should want positively to *emphasise* its importance for those in stressful jobs or positions of leadership where others make constant demands on them. Those 'private' times in our own home, for an individual, a couple or a family, are God's gift to us: they must be valued and guarded. Having said all that, I have to add that we can easily adopt a kind of siege mentality about our homes. I myself have been guilty of this. Following a serious illness, the most stressful thing was coping with people, particularly in large numbers. So home became the place of safe retreat, where nobody could get at me. (Our teenage children called it 'the old heart-attack ploy'!) That was a wise and very necessary precaution. But such a comfortable way of living can easily become a fixed mentality: we regard home as, essentially and only, a place of withdrawal.

I fear this will not do; we must remain open to the possibility of being called to use our homes, like all God's other gifts, sacrificially in his service. I know – and greatly admire – Christians who take in people in need, aware that they may become semi-permanent guests. The cost to family in such cases can be considerable – but so too may the mutual blessing sometimes be. Mostly the call will be less demanding, involving one-off visits, or maybe just a deliberate decision to invite unbelieving friends or neighbours in occasionally.

There may be someone reading this who would love to use their home in this way – if only they had one. Perhaps you are in residential care, or bed and breakfast accommodation; maybe you share someone else's home – or are even without any roof over your head. If so, please do not be irritated by what you have read. I hope you are receiving from Christians around you the special love and understanding – and practical support – you need. But for all who do have a home, whether it is one room or a large house, the question is valid, 'Am I prepared for the sacrifice involved in using my place to meet and share with others?' Remember that mysterious but challenging verse in Hebrews, 'Do not forget to entertain strangers, for by so doing some people have entertained angels without knowing it' (Heb 13:2).

* * *

The eminent 19th-century MP, William Wilberforce, led the great anti-slavery campaign which cost him his fortune, and the friendship and respect of his peers. Ending his life in comparative poverty, he said, 'A man can be as happy without a fortune as with one'. I am sure we all see the point, even though his life was quite unlike yours or mine.

I cannot put myself in your shoes. The challenges and questions I have posed are at best an arbitrary selection; I have no idea how relevant they might be to you. Even so, I pray that they may have prompted you to think afresh – or perhaps for the first time – about your lifestyle in the light of Christ's call to self-denial. Let the Holy Spirit prompt you to face the challenges and questions *you* ought to address in *your* circumstances. Let him lead you to answers which are right for you, and your family if you have one. And pray that he may give you the courage and resolve to follow where he leads. Costly obedience is always the way to blessing and real happiness.

> Only the man who follows the command of Jesus single-mindedly, and unresistingly lets his yoke rest upon him, finds his burden easy, and under its gentle pressure receives the power to persevere in the right way . . . Jesus asks nothing of us without giving us the strength to perform it. His commandment never seeks to destroy life, but to foster, strengthen and heal it.
> (Dietrich Bonhoeffer)[17]

ELEVEN
DYING TO SELF – THE BIG ISSUE

Be imitators of God, therefore, as dearly loved children and live a life of love, just as Christ loved us and gave himself up for us as a fragrant offering and sacrifice to God.
(Eph 5:1–2)

Through him we offer you our souls and bodies to be a living sacrifice. Send us out in the power of your Spirit to live and work to your praise and glory.
(ASB: Holy Communion Rite A)

In this book I have tried to explore some practical implications of Christ's call to self-sacrifice in relation to issues that face us in today's world. I am sure readers will have reacted in widely varying ways to what I have written. But one thing is certainly true for us all: we can only work out in our lives what is already inside. It is tragically easy to divorce daily living both from our worship – Amos (chapters 5 and 6) and Jesus (Mark 12:38–40) among others warn about that – and from an (otherwise admirable) concentration on the correctness of our belief. But 'Christian life is not primarily a ritual celebration, nor merely an intellectual adherence to a body of truths; it is primarily a participation in Christ by means of personal commitment to an active life of service and self-giving love'.[1] Our aim should be for living totally consistent with our believing and worshipping. A commonly-used prayer says:

'Grant, O Lord, that what we have said and sung with our lips we may believe in our hearts, and what we believe in our hearts we may show forth in our lives . . .'

So, then, this book will have failed if readers approve of what it contains (or even only some of it) but do not actually *do* anything. (See James 1:22–24.) Likewise, it will have missed its mark if it has convinced you that a greater readiness for self-sacrifice is, indeed, what Christians need today – *other* Christians, that is! However clear the promise that the way to find life is to lose it for Christ's sake (Matt 10:39), when it comes to the crunch none of us naturally wants to do it. We are inclined to disbelieve it, which is a repeat of Adam's original sin; or to 'believe' it in our mind without it working through our will to determine the way we live. Jesus said belief without action amounts to the same thing as unbelief (Matt 7:24–27).

> However convincingly the case is put that dying to self is the way to abundant life, there is something deep inside us that is sure we are bound to lose out by it.

So, in this final chapter, I have to ask you to join me in turning our eyes inwards. This will

Dying to Self – The Big Issue

certainly be challenging. It may be painful. If we responded negatively to some of the practical sacrificial issues explored earlier, we might trace the source of that reaction. We might uncover areas deep within our mind, emotions or will which have not yet been yielded to Christ's loving invasion of our lives. I say 'we', because at this point readers and writer are travelling along the same road together. I share any shame or pain you may feel – writing this book has itself been an arduous journey inwards.

* * *

Before we go any further, I must make an important distinction. It is vital that it is appreciated; otherwise, the whole of this chapter (or, indeed, the book) is liable to be misunderstood.

Self-Denial is not Self-Destruction

Brought up among Strict Baptists, I used to sing a hymn by Isaac Watts beginning:

> Great God! how infinite art thou!
> What worthless worms are we!

I get the (scriptural) allusions – and there is truth in the thought. Looking back, though, I see that it was part of a whole 'theology of worthlessness'. Now, years later, I am certain that believers for whom Christ died have no business to speak of themselves in such disparaging terms. At the very heart of the Christian faith lies a resounding affirmation of the immense worth of the individual. The call to 'die to self' must never be understood as a call to self-destruction. God has made you and me unique. We are so infinitely precious to him that he sent his Son to die for us. Moreover, his word assures us that we shall stand with the redeemed before his throne *as ourselves*, resurrected but recognizable, changed but not replaced (Job 19:26–27; 2 Cor 3:18).

Dying to self is a process, not a single event. True, meeting Christ brings dramatic change to some people: few more so than Paul, yet he still struggled with the 'old nature' (Rom 7:7–25). His theology of being 'crucified with Christ' means putting the 'old man' to death. He describes this not as destroying, but liberating, the 'new man' which is the Christian's *true* self – 'that we should no longer be slaves to sin – because anyone who has died has been freed from sin' (Rom 6:6–7). The purpose is equally clear: 'I no longer live, but Christ lives in me. The life I live in the body, I live by faith in the Son of God, who loved me and gave himself for me' (Gal 2:20). (This is further expounded in Galatians 5:24; Romans 8:9–11 and 1 Peter 4:1–2.) The purpose of progressive death to self is to enable the progressive growth of Christ's life in us. 'He must become greater; I must become less' (John 3:30). This is immensely positive. The whole purpose of our existence is to grow in Christ-likeness, with the ultimate promise that when Christ appears we shall be 'like him' (1 John 3:2). This puts the matter beyond any doubt.

> The call to self-sacrifice as the essence of discipleship is emphatically NOT about self-destruction. It is the irrefutable proof of our self-worth: God loves each one of us enough to be concerned that we grow towards our ultimate destiny of complete likeness to his own, dearly-loved Son.

Dying to Self – The Big Issue 215

A partial or total loss of self-worth lies behind much of the individual and communal malaise afflicting our society today. Cut off from what was (wrongly) seen as the restricting notion that we are created by and for God, millions are adrift with no idea who they are or why they are here. The Christian faith, with its emphasis on the infinite value of the individual, is the only antidote to this condition of lostness. We should be careful never to render it ineffective by confusing self-denial with self-worthlessness. As Ian Bradley says, '[Sacrifice] is not about self-punishment or self-abasement but is about growing in our discipleship through self-denial and limitation . . . The whole concept of sacrifice is founded on the notion of individual self-worth'.[2]

* * *

Having established that, we must now consider some of the remnants of the old nature which spoil our discipleship and mar the image of God in us, and which must therefore be 'put to death'. 'The image of God is the image of Christ crucified. It is to this image that the life of the disciples must be conformed: in other words they must be conformed to his death'.[3] Since Christ's image is essentially *self-sacrificial*, it should not surprise us that the things to which we must die are all essentially *self-centred*.

Self-Importance

In the Old Testament, Naaman almost missed being healed of leprosy through self-importance

(2 Kings 5). In the New Testament, James and John got more than they bargained for when they presumptuously tried to book the best seats in Christ's (earthly, as they thought) kingdom – and received the promise of martyrdom. The apostles Paul and Peter understood this temptation: 'Do not think of yourself more highly than you ought' (Rom 12:3); 'All of you, clothe yourselves with humility towards one another' (1 Pet 5:5). In story and precept, the Bible consistently outlaws self-importance. It is one of the ugliest manifestations of the un-crucified 'I' still occupying centre stage. It lies behind most un-sacrificial behaviour. It appears in various guises. Here are some:

The 'King-Pin' Mentality

Many of us think we are indispensable. Leaders especially (but not exclusively) can have a real problem of unrealistic self-image. The legacy still lingers of the ignorant laity led by the omnicompetent parson, the only one in the community who could even read or write! It is partly nourished by the unrealistic expectations some parishioners still have of their clergy; the mismatch between this and the mainly theological training clergy receive is stark. In the 1990s, is the ordained leader necessarily the best person to chair the Church Council, meet the architect, edit the magazine, purchase office machinery . . . ? God's work can actually be held back or damaged by a leader who insists on doing himself what others could do more effectively. Leaders who think they must be a 'superman' in order to earn the respect of their flock must learn to sacrifice this unrealistic self-image. Doing so is like taking the cork out of the bottle: it commonly unlocks the gifts of others in a church and is the gateway to renewal of its life and witness.

The Desire for Power

This too affects leaders, but by no means only them. The desire to exercise power over others can colour — and sometimes govern — anyone's relationships, though they are rarely conscious of it. It may underlie the actions of that person who is always doing things for people. In other words, it can be the 'dark side' of lives that look as if they are lived for others. Apparently self-effacing service may hide self-assertion, the desire to be important in other people's lives, even to control them. In close personal relationships this attitude can be very damaging. Here is a litmus test to apply to ourselves. Do we find it easy to receive what others have to give? If not, it probably indicates that we value relationships mainly for the opportunity they give us to dominate, with little appreciation of the intrinsic value of other people.[4] I recognise that such a personality may stem from experiences early in life, making it very deep-seated and 'not our fault'. Nevertheless, the scriptures about valuing, esteeming and honouring others above ourselves suggest it needs to be brought to God in prayer for his healing touch.

The Desire to be Right

Some Christians appear to derive satisfaction — even their security — from being right. And not only *being* right, but *proving* they're right! Evangelicals, especially, seem to love bandying words: the letters pages of the Christian press display this compulsion. An essential part of being right seems to be proving others wrong — sometimes in a distressingly aggressive spirit. Naturally, all concerned use scripture to support their views – even about matters of order rather than faith or doctrine. This may seem like fair game to some. To me it appears as a lack of self-restraint in a whole important area of the personality – the intellect. Defending the truth *for truth's sake* is one thing – vitally necessary in the face of liberalism in some quarters, and subjective, virtually doctrine-less, Christianity in others. But that is quite different from contending for our own perceptions, as if our very status as God's children depends on our 'being right', rather than on his undeserved grace and mercy. Intellectual superiority is a far cry from the New Testament's summons to humility, forbearance and love towards fellow-believers. This has always been a dangerous sin; recent controversies in the Church of England have brought it to the fore. 'Quarrelling about words . . . is of no value' (2 Tim 2:14). Contentiousness belongs to the old nature: it is a form of spiritual self-indulgence which needs to be repented of.

Self-Sufficiency

I suspect we all have one or more areas of our life where we try to keep God out. Maybe we just do not see our faith as relevant to them – some people think that about money. But perhaps they are precisely the areas which we know are self-centred, and we do not want them shown up or interfered with. These may well include, for example, our sexuality, relationships or indifference to social problems.

Dying to Self – The Big Issue

Keeping life in separate compartments, perhaps under two broad headings 'believing' and 'living', can be convenient and comfortable. Believing can be mainly about intellectual assent to the tenets of Christianity; we may invest considerable effort in tying down our beliefs in a neat doctrinal package. I do not mean this as a caricature. Indeed, it is highly desirable that more Christians 'correctly handle the word of truth' (2 Tim 2:15). But there is a frame of mind which I can best describe as a kind of closed-circuit Christianity. It goes something like this: 'All truth is contained in the Bible, and I have studied and got a grasp of all the doctrine, so I do not have to do anything more'. People with this mentality tend to read only books by authors who are 'sound', i.e., will reinforce their own outlook. They do not expect, or want, to be confronted with new aspects of truth, or new angles on how truth interfaces with life. They retreat behind set formulae, or a trenchant 'anyway, that's what God's word says'. Not for them the difficult, at times virtually impenetrable, territory where God's written word meets modern life – like *in-vitro* fertilisation, ethical investment, environmental responsibility or faith in a multi-cultural society. What is more, they are inclined to view with suspicion those who do grapple with such issues. It is vital that we work to establish a truly biblical perspective on modern life, and sad when well-taught Christians refuse to sacrifice the personal security of the trenches for the open ground where the way they believe would be tested against the demands and challenges of life in a secular world.

A similar detachment may be observed among Christians whose faith is expressed not in terms of doctrine but of their 'worship experiences'. I

heard recently about a college where most of the
Christian Union are charismatic to the core – but
they might as well be on another planet! And,
of course, there have always been staid, regular
churchgoers of a reserved disposition whose 'religion
is a private matter between me and God' and who
'don't mix my Christianity up with everyday life'. All
these folk have, in slightly different ways, hung a
notice on their door saying 'Do not disturb – religion
in progress'. In a sermon preached while he was
Archbishop of Canterbury, Donald Coggan said:

> This Man who talks about taking up a cross
> and going to be crucified, who assaults the will
> much more than the emotions, who touches
> the roots of a man's obedience and even takes
> over the mastery of his cheque book – that's
> quite another thing.[5]

Another false security needing to be sacrificed
is the tendency to cut God down to the limits
of our ability to comprehend him. Yes, we can
know God: Christ has revealed him to us – and
that in itself is amazing. But we are seriously
mistaken if we suppose that the sum total of all
our theologising, praying, worshipping and daily
living adds up to – God. In fact, we are more
like people looking through a keyhole: we can see
enough to know that the room beyond the door
is a vast, richly-furnished hall, but 95 per cent
of it is outside our field of vision. J. B. Phillips'
book title 'Your God is Too Small' is a needful
reminder to us all. If we are not careful we can
spend so much time chopping logic as if our very
lives depended on it – and as though, if we can
only get the words right to describe and define

him, then that *is* God. We need to be reminded that 'all that we affirm concerning God, however correct, falls far short of the living truth'.[6] We *can* know all we *need* to know to find saving faith and live Christianly in his world – but let us never suppose that is all there *is* to know. An element of reverent agnosticism is a healthy antidote to spiritual pride.

Self-Satisfaction

Let me say at once that Christians *should* be at peace with themselves. Often we are not: even though we may know in our hearts that God accepts us, we find it much harder to accept ourselves. We need to learn self-acceptance. But that is a quite different thing from spiritual self-satisfaction – or, in a word, pride. This can be seen in many forms. Here are some:

(1) *Spiritual pedigree*. My antennae tend to quiver when the first thing a person wants to tell me on meeting them is that they grew up in St —'s, —, or (worse still) 'in (*well-known minister*)'s church'. In some circles, certain churches and leaders serve as buzz-words to identify 'where you are coming from', or even to attempt to boost your image. I know – I've caught myself doing it! But we ought not to think like that. That kind of thing ('I'm in Paul's house group') was first among the signs of spiritual immaturity that Paul criticised in his hard-hitting letter to Corinth (1 Cor 1:10–17). This attitude – in effect a spiritual ghetto mentality – can be quite damaging. Seeing our identity in terms of one branch of one tradition in one denomination seriously limits our openness

to what God might ask of us. I always admire a leader who perceives, and has the courage to follow, God's call to serve outside the tradition he or she has been used to. Which matters more – the needs of the gospel or our own desire to stay where we feel comfortable? Paul set a sterling example: a prize graduate from the right university, taught by the famous Gamaliel, he put all that aside to become like a Jew to Jews, under the law for those under the law, weak to those who were weak – in fact 'a slave to everyone . . . so that by all possible means I might save some' (1 Cor 9:19–23).

(2) *Spiritual superiority.* This has always been with us, and will be while the Devil is loose. It is one of the chief, if not *the* chief, means he uses to spoil our discipleship. 'Any growth in faith will only be possible if we can openly come to terms with our great enemy, the ego . . . The first step in humility is to recognize the pride of self, and simply ask God for help.'[7] We can become proud of our Bible knowledge, our prayer life, our holiness, the size of 'our' congregation – the variety of avenues through which this temptation can come is almost endless. Today, as in 1st-century Corinth, some Christians with particular spiritual gifts look down on those without them. Even sacrifice itself can become a 'luxury', something we enjoy talking about, deriving a smug satisfaction from its effects on our life. (This is rather like the hypocrites with their prayer and fasting – Matt 6:5, 16–18 . . . and Dickens' 'very 'umble' Uriah Heep: 'I'm a very sacrificial Christian'!) Augustine of Hippo, writing almost 1600 years ago, reminds us that 'even the mercy we show to men, if it is not shown for God's sake, is not a sacrifice'.

(3) *The desire to be admired.* It would be salutary

Dying to Self – The Big Issue

to stop in the middle of our Christian work sometimes and ask ourselves, 'How much of this am I doing to impress others?' This is especially important for people with 'upfront' roles. More than once in my years as a church musician I have been faced with this question – and been ashamed at the answer I had to give. Leaders of any kind may easily become motivated in part by the desire for recognition. They need constantly to ask before God how much of their very hard work and busyness are in fact about sacrificial service, and how much about maintaining the esteem in which they are held. 'Successful' Christian ministers can be among the most driven people. Where a very full engagements diary allows them too little time to be still, listening and prayerful, it may be to the detriment of their own spiritual health and growth – and therefore, ultimately, also of that ministry to others which they see as their 'sacrificial' service. In that case a full diary is a matter for self-examination, and possibly repentance, rather than pride.

(4) *Being satisfied with a hidden or shallow faith*. I keep returning to the call not to be conformed to the world's image, but to be transformed. That should make Christians different – at times *very* different – from those around them. I was always surprised when it emerged that somebody I had known for years at work was a Christian, but I had never realised it – and ashamed to think that they presumably never knew that I was. How often we stop short of positively identifying ourselves as Christ's men and women. It cannot be because the need to do so never arises – life is just not like that! It must be because we put higher priority on keeping the liking and respect of colleagues

or neighbours. At times it may go rather deeper, as when we deliberately play down or hide our Christian commitment because it might damage our prospects. So often we are satisfied with that level of commitment. Yet in truth

> . . . a life which is intended to be sacrificial . . . is a life which really will be characterised by personal disadvantage . . . It can mean a life which to the world's judgement may appear unsuccessful; it can also mean the loss of self-esteem through the dispiriting fact of marginalisation . . . We are, nevertheless, called to be fools for Christ's sake . . .[8]

Of course, it may not often come to a critical point for most of us. But there are many small instances daily where our visible allegiance to Christ is compromised by self-satisfaction with a level of open commitment which costs us little.

Self-Pity

A very good friend characterises this, very aptly, as not only a 'no hope' but also a 'no cope' generation. This can be seen in all kinds of ways – from the demands for compensation for every kind of loss (real or imagined) to the idea that you need counselling if you stub your toe! Some people bear heavy burdens of responsibility and suffering. Examples abound of those who do so cheerfully and without fuss. We should recognise their immense courage and draw inspiration from them. But most stories that make the media suggest that, compared with previous generations, we

Dying to Self – The Big Issue

tend today to fall apart at the first sign of trouble. Being a Christian should make a difference here. For several reasons, we ought to react quite differently to trouble, and not retreat into 'whingers' corner' with the rest.

(1) *Christ told his followers to expect trouble.* 'In this world you will have trouble. But take heart! I have overcome the world' (John 16:33). He had told them that some troubles (insults and persecution) were evidence of their heavenward-bound faith (Matt 5:11–12). This may not sound very convincing to our ears in 1990s Britain. But down the centuries it has been the inspiration for many martyrs for Christ, and still is in some places today. I am told that in Australia it is now a criminal offence to criticise publicly any 'alternative lifestyle' – a kind of repressive liberalism! A Christian leader there has suggested people will take notice of us again when we start going to prison for our Christian stance. It may be that in Britain the true strength of recent renewal will yet be tested by trials of kind which have not arisen for centuries. If so, may God 'strengthen [us] with power through his Spirit in [our] inner being' (Eph 3:16).

(2) *We can draw on God's strength and know his presence.* Paul's affliction (thorn in the flesh) caused him real agony, but he treasured God's promise in answer to his prayers, 'My grace is sufficient for you, for my strength is made perfect in weakness.' Another friend of ours once made the encouraging suggestion that limits to my own health might be regarded as a gift – a 'ministry of weakness'. Perhaps some such thought enabled Paul to say that he was actually glad about his weaknesses, 'so that Christ's power may rest on me. That is why, for Christ's sake,

I delight in weaknesses, in insults, in hardships, in persecutions, in difficulties. For when I am weak, then I am strong' (2 Cor 12:7–10). We can know Christ with us in our troubles in a very special way. One of the 'by-products' of his Incarnation is that he *understands*, not just from outside, but from inside the human condition. 'We do not have a high priest who is unable to sympathise with our weaknesses . . . Because he himself suffered when he was tempted, he is able to help those who are being tempted.' That is why we can be confident of finding 'grace to help us in our time of need' (Heb 4:15–16; 2:18).

(3) *We can see God's loving purpose in trouble*. Discipline (through 'hardship') 'produces a harvest of righteousness and peace for those who have been trained by it' (Heb 12:11). Paul sets out an increasingly-positive 'chain-reaction': 'suffering produces perseverance; perseverance, character; and character, hope. And hope does not disappoint us' (Rom 5:3–5). Despite his frustration that his own affliction seemed to him to limit his work for God, he recognised its purpose in keeping him from becoming conceited (2 Cor 12:7). Of course doubts sometimes assail us. But as God's children we can *know* beyond any doubt that in all that God allows into our life he has a loving purpose. That purpose, though, may not always be evident to us at the time – and it may not relate to this life at all.

(4) *We can see trouble in an eternal perspective*. I made much in Chapter Two of the dangers of being 'earthbound.' As well as making us hold too tightly to this life's joys, it may cause us to make heavy weather of its sorrows. The eternal

perspective is an antidote for both maladies. If Paul was tempted to self-pity, he took the long view and reckoned that 'our present sufferings are not worth comparing with the glory that will be revealed in us' (Rom 8:18). In that light, he asserts that: 'We are hard pressed on every side, but not crushed; perplexed, but not in despair; persecuted, but not abandoned; struck down, but not destroyed' (2 Cor 4:8–9).

Christians are weak human beings just like everyone else. But I hope it is clear that I am not just advocating a sanctified stiff upper lip. I have suggested reasons why, when trouble strikes, there is no place for 'why should this happen to me?', or even 'poor little me'. The Father's reassurance, the Son's presence, and the Spirit's power are always available to us. All this should enable us to sacrifice the indulgence of self-pity as we grow in grace.

Self-Indulgence

Every Christian experiences temptation. It affects even those leading a cloistered existence of prayer and contemplation; to imagine otherwise is a mistake. The constant battle between the new nature and the old is an inherent part of being a Christian. So we should not be surprised because we continue to sin. But we must mourn the sins themselves, ever aware that they pierce the Father's heart of love, and give pain to Christ who died for us. And they grieve the Spirit, whose work in our life is not just to bring joy and distribute gifts, but includes cleansing. He is the *Holy* Spirit. The New Testament's many exhortations to holiness must be taken seriously. The Christian who takes sin lightly has reason to be deeply concerned about his or her spiritual state.

Bonhoeffer referred to those who think their sins are forgiven simply because they 'leave the world for an hour or so on Sunday morning and go to church'. Attacking the ethos of 'cheap grace' with great emotion and intensity, he says:

> . . . the world finds a cheap covering for its sins; no contrition is required, still less any real desire to be delivered from sin. Cheap grace therefore amounts to a denial of the living Word of God, in fact, a denial of the Incarnation of the Word of God.[9]

That was written in the Germany of the 1930s. I cannot think that the sense of sin goes any deeper in society — or, indeed, sometimes in the Church — in 1990s Britain. Those of us who preach and teach must take our share of blame for the generally low level of awareness of 'the exceeding sinful[ness]' of sin (Rom 7:13) among Christians today. Intent on proclaiming God's love, we so easily forget, or gloss over, his holiness.

As individuals this applies most pointedly to our besetting sins. You have them — so do I. The question is: as the Holy Spirit has revealed them to me, and convicted me of them, have I faced up to the need to let them go — to sacrifice the pleasure, satisfaction or profit they provide? The New Testament contains fearful warnings about the dangers of deliberately continuing in sin. In Romans 6 Paul demolishes the argument that we may continue sinning because God's love and grace are inexhaustible. (They are, thank God:

Dying to Self – The Big Issue

there is 'grace to cover all my sin', but that is to put the statement the other way round.) John's first epistle is full of the love and forgiveness of God; yet he writes uncompromisingly about those who 'keep on sinning' – that is, wilfully cling on to sin, fully aware that that is what they are doing (1 John 3:4–10). Hebrews 10:26–31 contains some of the most challenging teaching of the whole New Testament: deliberately continuing in open sin which amounts to a rejection of the gospel, and therefore of Christ who died for us, leaves us in a state where 'no [other] sacrifice for sins is left, but only a fearful expectation of judgment'.

These are solemn warnings. We ignore them at our peril. Just as we take a conscious decision to place our faith in Jesus as our Saviour, so God requires of us a conscious decision to turn away from repeated sin of which we are aware. That is an inherent and continuing part of sacrificial living – of answering Christ's call to take up our cross and follow him. 'Life is marked by a daily dying in the war between the flesh and the spirit . . . This is the suffering of Christ which all his disciples on earth must undergo'.[10]

Although the more subtle sins may lie hidden for years until the Spirit reveals them to us, the marks which distinguish Christian from worldly living are clear. Few things are sadder than a Christian who normally handles God's word honestly manipulating it to justify his or her own particular sins (probably toned down to 'weaknesses'). In Galatians 5 Paul listed typical acts of the sinful nature, and contrasted them with the fruit of the Spirit. Then came the unequivocal challenge to holy living: 'Those who belong to Christ Jesus have crucified the sinful nature with its passions and desires. Since we live by the Spirit, let us keep in step with the Spirit' (Gal 5:24–25). Although it is a continuing process, he uses the past tense: '*have* crucified'. Not for him – or us – Augustine's prayer that God would make him holy . . . but not yet. Scripture has some examples of deliberate letting-go. Job, obviously suffering one of the commonest besetting sins, said, 'I made a covenant with my eyes not to look lustfully at a girl' (Job 31:1). We can determine, with God's help, not to go into situations where we are likely to fall. Angry people – don't nurse your anger overnight: that only enables the devil to take hold of your sinful tendency and make things worse (Eph 4:26–27). Then there was Zacchaeus, the tax man, who not only cleaned up his act and stopped cheating, but repaid his victims – by more than the law required. Making good the harm our sin has done to others (where this is possible) may be an additional sacrifice – letting go not just of the pleasure or profit of the sin itself, but also of our dignity and self-esteem.

Self-Will

The will is the centre of our being, the part of us which actually moves us to do, or not to do, things. We are all familiar with those times when mind or emotions – or maybe both together – urge us to some particular course of action. We *know* and *feel* it is right. But we do not do it. The road to hell is paved with good intentions, says the old proverb. The gap between our best intentions and our actions represents those parts of our will which have not been surrendered sacrificially to

Dying to Self – The Big Issue

God. John Drinkwater's prayerful poem says it precisely:

> Grant us the will to fashion as we feel,
> Grant us the strength to labour as we know,
> Grant us the purpose, ribb'd and edged with steel,
> To strike the blow.
>
> Knowledge we ask not – knowledge thou hast lent,
> But Lord, the will – there lies our bitter need,
> Give us to build above the deep intent.
>   The deed, the deed.[11]

It was the surrender of man's *will* which caused the Fall. Both the logic of the mind ('we could be like God') and the desire of the emotions (it was 'pleasant to the eye') were involved. But it was in willing the action, reaching out and taking the forbidden fruit, that mankind fell. Through the will's disobedience sin entered into our very nature, shattering God's image in us. When, through Christ 'the second Adam', that image is restored, and the mind and emotions are turned back to God, the will is the last bastion to be surrendered. It is here that the 'I' in each of us holds out, refusing to let go of that deep-rooted conviction that ultimately 'it's my own life'. For the Christian that is simply not true. It is Satan's great lie. 'You are not your own; you were bought at a price' (1 Cor 6:19–20). As the theologian Karl Barth said, 'Each is to climb down from the throne on which he sits'.

What then shall we do? What *can* we do, except recognise our need honestly and throw ourselves on God's mercy? This was just what Paul felt as he surveyed the battle between the old and new natures that was his life. 'Wretched man!' he said, 'who will rescue me?' But he did not leave it there, but burst out, 'Thanks be to God – through Jesus Christ our Lord' (Rom 7:24–25). All the power of God is available to every Christian through the indwelling of the Holy Spirit.

> I pray that out of his glorious riches he may strengthen you with power through his Spirit in your inner being . . .
>
> That power is like the working of his mighty strength, which he exerted in Christ when he raised him from the dead and seated him at his right hand in the heavenly realms.
> (Eph 3:16; 1:19–20)

If the life of self-sacrifice glimpsed in this book seems impossible, then this will sound like amazingly good news. It is; but I do not include it as the obligatory happy ending! In order to experience this power in our lives, we must lay our whole selves – heart, mind and will – totally open before God, allowing him to show us where the un-yielded parts are, and being prepared to sacrifice them. This will be a continuous, often painful, process. It will take a lifetime. But a positive, immediate start would be to take some of the prayer time we usually spend asking God for things, and make it over consciously to this process of opening up our lives to him. For those who attend Holy Communion where the liturgy ends with the prayer 'Through him we offer you our souls and bodies

Dying to Self – The Big Issue

to be a living sacrifice', why not make that a conscious moment of personal re-dedication to the sacrificial life of discipleship?

As the Holy Spirit enables us to become progressively more open to self-sacrifice, the most tangible results are likely to be in our relationships; for these are usually the main arena for (maybe unconscious) self-centredness. The effects will start to be felt in our home, marriage, family, church, community, work – every context, in fact, that we have already considered in this book and, certainly, some that we have not.

But increasing self-sacrifice will, of course, also have an impact on the whole direction of our life. It will highlight, perhaps as never before, the central question, 'What am I doing with my life – following my own devices, or seeking and following God's will?' That question arises unmistakably at key points in our lives – choosing a marriage partner, changing jobs, moving home. But it also underlies one-hundred-and-one lesser, but still vital, decisions. In these, and in all the minutiae of daily living, the process of 'climbing down from the throne on which we sit' moves us, however gradually, along a line which starts from

it's my own life, and I don't really see where God or religion come into things like that

towards

I am praying that my will may become so closely aligned with God's that I desire only those things he wills for me.

Or, as Katie Wilkinson put it:

> May the mind of Christ my Saviour
> Live in me from day to day,
> By his love and power controlling
> All I do and say.[12]

Most Christians will already be somewhere along the line between those two extremes. The important thing is not so much how far we have got, but that we keep – or get – moving. Then we shall be walking the pathway that Jesus walked as he 'stedfastly set his face to go to Jerusalem' (Luke 9:51 KJV). We shall join him on the way of the Cross, moving with him towards the final surrender expressed in the words, 'Not as I will, but as you will'. For him, on that one occasion in Gethsemane, those words were crucial for the salvation of mankind. For us, too, wherever and however often we say them, they may be the most crucial words we can utter. For it is in total surrender that we show our willingness for the demands of true discipleship, so that we can say with Paul:

> I have been crucified with Christ and I no longer live, but Christ lives in me. The life I live in the body, I live by faith in the Son of God, who loved me and gave himself for me.
> (Gal 2:20)

EPILOGUE

The Church of England's Rite A Holy Communion service contains a beautiful closing prayer thanking God that in Jesus he has 'brought us home'. It contains the phrase

Dying and living, he declared your love . . .

When we try to sum up someone's existence, we say 'she lived and died a keen gardener . . .' or whatever it might be. But the prayer does not say 'living and dying'; it says 'dying and living'. That is striking, beautiful — and, in the context of our subject in this book, full of significance.

Has the message of self-sacrifice seemed negative — over-demanding — heavy — gloomy — life-denying? If so, we are probably looking through the wrong end of the telescope. We are thinking in terms of living and dying. But followers of Christ can, and should, think of dying and living — *in that order!* He said: '. . . whoever loses his life for me will find it' (Matt 16:25).

That is the principle which applies here and now. Dying to self means constantly and repeatedly setting aside our 'rights' and our own 'self-fulfilment' for the good of others and for God's glory. That — if we will only believe and do it — is the way to discover our *real* rights (the right to be called children of God) and *real* self-fulfilment

('I no longer live, but Christ lives in me'). Even in this life, dying is the way to real living.

But if we take the long view, our destiny is not to live and then die – but to die (physically) and then live (eternally). That is the view we *must* take. The Risen Christ's great gift to us is the absolute certainty of life after death. It is only as we see our *whole* life, here and hereafter, as a single piece, that we see anything in true perspective. Then we really can see self-sacrifice, dying to self – not just in principle but as we actually seek to practise it – not as an heavy imposition, but an astounding privilege. It is the process by which God lovingly, if at times painfully, is making us more like the image of Christ, who died and rose again for us, and now intercedes for us. If we go with that process, it will lead without fail to its amazing fulfilment, when Christ comes back, and we are made completely like him, fit to spend eternity praising him and reigning with him. Incredible – but true!

I don't know about you – but I'm just DYING TO LIVE!

NOTES

Introduction

1. Dietrich Bonhoeffer (translated by R H Fuller/Irmgard Booth), *The Cost of Discipleship* (London: SCM Press, 1959).
2. Ibid p 50.
3. Ian Bradley, *The Power of Sacrifice* (London: Darton, Longman & Todd, 1995).
4. Ibid p vii.

Prologue: Sacrifice . . . ? You Can't Mean Me!

1. This is the main thrust of Ian Bradley's book (op. cit). He shows how sacrifice, written into the way the universe functions, is of the very essence of the life of God himself, and consequently of the life he calls us to share.

   > Sacrifice is indeed, the way, the truth and the life. It is not some unfortunate burden that we have to shoulder because of our sin but rather the basis of our lives as creatures made by God, redeemed by Christ and living under his Cross . . . The sacrifice of Christ . . . is the decisive expression of the underlying principle which animates the whole of God's work of creation, redemption and perfection through which he draws all to himself and makes all holy. (p 135)

Chapter 1: The Call to Sacrifice

1. William Barclay, *The Gospel of Matthew (Revised ed.)* (Philadelphia, Westminster Press, 1975) ii, p 151.
2. In *The Power of Sacrifice* (op. cit), Ian Bradley draws on a wide variety of sources to show how, rightly understood, God's act of creation as well as of redemption involves self-sacrifice. The result of this, he argues, is that the principle of self-sacrifice is built into the very structure of the universe – there is always a death preceding new life. (cf the sowing and reaping idea in John 12:23ff and 1 Corinthians 15:42–44.) Writing of the Cross, William Temple pointed to a relationship of self-giving love within the Trinity (Bradley, p 209), foreshadowing late 20th-century theologians in opening up new insights into the 'suffering of God'. Bradley summarises Jurgen Moltmann: 'The Son suffers death in dereliction; the Father suffers the death of his Son in the pain of his love. Each is forsaken and given up by the other. Yet they are also brought together by the Cross in their common sacrifice. In surrendering his Son, the Father surrenders himself. He is both forsaking and forsaken' (Bradley, pp 218–9). He himself refers to the costly and painful sacrificial love revealed in the Cross as 'the dynamic which moves and powers the Trinity' (p 266).
3. Sadly, it is not easy amongst those who would call themselves Christians to reach agreement even on such an apparently fundamental matter as defining what a Christian is. But I hope this minimalist attempt will be generally acceptable! See John 3:16–18, 36; 1 John 5:12; Acts 2:38.
4. Dietrich Bonhoeffer, *The Cost of Discipleship*, op. cit. p 79.
5. Ian Bradley, *The Power of Sacrifice*, op. cit. p 213.

6. Dietrich Bonhoeffer, *The Cost of Discipleship*, op. cit. p 78.
7. J.I. Packer, *Laid-Back Religion?* (Leicester, Inter-Varsity Press, 1987) p 53.
8. Ibid p 54.
9. Dietrich Bonhoeffer, *The Cost of Discipleship*, op. cit. p 77.

Chapter 2: The Context of Sacrifice

1. From Charles Wesley's hymn 'Love divine, all loves excelling', to be found in all standard hymn books.
2. Wild Goose Worship Group, *A Wee Worship Book* (Glasgow, Wild Goose Worship Group, 1990) p 13. This prayer is included in one of a number of Morning Liturgies in this most helpful book.
3. Charles Wesley's hymn 'Love's redeeming work is done' (appears in some hymnals under its original first verse 'Christ the Lord is risen today').
4. Ian Bradley, *The Power of Sacrifice*, op. cit. p 45.
5. J.I. Packer, *Laid-Back Religion?*, op. cit. p 58. The whole of Chapter 4 (entitled 'Hot Tub Religion') of this book expounds fully and clearly Dr Packer's view that the almost wholly 'this world' perspective in contemporary thought poses a serious danger to Christians.
6. Ibid pp 62–3.
7. Dietrich Bonhoeffer, *The Cost of Discipleship*, op. cit. p 99.
8. Ibid p 79.
9. Ian Bradley, *The Power of Sacrifice*, op. cit. p 301.
10. Martyn Lloyd-Jones, *Studies in the Sermon on the Mount* (One-Volume Edition) (Leicester, Inter-Varsity Press, 1976) p 118.
11. From A Bloom, *God and Man* (Darton, Longman & Todd, 1971), quoted by Ian Bradley, op. cit. p 23.
12. From Charles Wesley's hymn 'O thou who camest from above', to be found in all standard hymn books.

13. Maria Boulding, *The Coming of God* (London, SPCK, 1982) p 82.
14. Ian Bradley, *The Power of Sacrifice*, op. cit. p 20.
15. From Isaac Watts' hymn 'When I survey the wondrous Cross', undoubtedly one of the few hymns to claim a place in the great classics of the heritage of the English language.

Chapter 3: Church Life – (1) The Sacrificial Pattern

1. From an article in *Alpha* magazine, December 1993. Quoted by Ian Bradley in *The Power of Sacrifice*, op. cit. p 290.
2. Maria Boulding, *The Coming of God*, op. cit. p 12.
3. Ibid p 17.
4. Helen Roseveare, *Living Sacrifice* (Hodder & Stoughton, London and Toronto, 1979) pp 24–8.

Chapter 4: Church Life – (2) Worship

1. John Leach, *Liturgy and Liberty* (Tunbridge Wells, MARC, 1989) p 245.
2. Derek Baldwin, *Open Doors Open Minds* (Guildford, Highland Books, 1994). This book tells the story of recent events in the life of St John's, Boscombe in Bournemouth, and how opening itself to the local community resulted in the church and people themselves being radically changed. On the question of the church and alcoholics see especially pp 150–8 and 211.
3. Ian Bradley, *The Power of Sacrifice*, op. cit. p 273.
4. Wild Goose Worship Group, *A Wee Worship Book*, op. cit. p 7.
5. John Leach, *Liturgy and Liberty*, op. cit. p 25.
6. John Leach, 'Fit to Worship' – an article in *Christian Music* magazine, Winter 1992, p12.
7. John Leach, *Liturgy and Liberty*, op. cit. p 101.

8. Derek Fathers, essay 'Family Communion in the Country Parish' in *Worship in a Changing Church*, ed. R.S. Wilkinson (Leighton Buzzard, Faith Press, 1965) pp 97–8.
9. I list below a small selection of the books which those coming new to this subject may find helpful:

    Paul Simmonds, *Reaching the Unchurched: some lessons from Willow Creek*, Grove Booklet on Evangelism No. 19 (Bramcote, Nottingham, Grove Books, 1992). A brief but good introductory resume.

    Martin Robinson, *A World Apart: Creating a Church for the Unchurched* (Tunbridge Wells, Monarch, 1992). A look at some British applications of the original American approach.

    Martin Robinson, *The Faith of the Unbeliever* (Tunbridge Wells, Monarch, 1994). Looks at background issues to preaching at 'seeker' events.

    A. Hibbert, *Creating a Church for the Unchurched* (Warwick, CPAS, 1992). Much helpful background, especially useful for communicating the concept to existing congregations.

    R. Sutton, *How to Preach at Seeker Services*: Church Leadership Pack No. 26 (Warwick, CPAS, 1995).
10. John Leach, *Liturgy and Liberty*, op. cit. p 253.
11. Ian Bradley, *The Power of Sacrifice*, op. cit. p 289.
12. Maria Boulding, *The Coming of God*, op. cit. p 19.

Chapter 5: Church Life – (3) Relationships

1. David Watson, *I Believe In The Church* (London, Hodder & Stoughton, 1978) p 82.
2. Ian Bradley, *The Power of Sacrifice*, op. cit. p 149.
3. H. M. Carson, *Colossians & Philemon* in *Tyndale New Testament Commentaries* (London, Inter-Varsity Press, 1960) p 88.
4. Michael Marshall, *Just Like Him* (London, The Bible Reading Fellowship, 1989) p 54.

5. Dietrich Bonhoeffer, *The Cost of Discipleship*, op. cit. pp 116–7.
6. Ian Bradley, *The Power of Sacrifice,* op. cit. p 245.
7. J. R. Laville, essay 'Gifts and Ministries in the Body of Christ', contained in *Christ's Living Body*, ed. John P Baker (London & Eastbourne, Coverdale House Publishers Ltd, 1973) p 112.
8. Ibid p 112.
9. David Prior, *Bedrock – Vision for the Local Church* (London, Hodder & Stoughton, 1985) pp 58–9.

Chapter 6: Church Life – (4) Outreach

1. Included in *A Treasury of Quotations on Christian Themes* (London, SPCK, 1976). The precise source is not identified.
2. *Faith in the City: The Report of the Archbishop of Canterbury's Commission on Urban Priority Areas* (London, Church House Publishing, 1985) paragraph 4.13, p 75.
3. See my book, *Open Doors Open Minds*, op. cit.
4. Dietrich Bonhoeffer, *The Cost of Discipleship*, op. cit. p 106.
5. David Watson, *I Believe In The Church*, op. cit. p 306.
6. Further details and information about Traidcraft can be obtained by writing to Traidcraft plc, Kingsway, GATESHEAD, Tyne & Wear, NE11 0NE (telephone 0191 491 0591).

Chapter 7: Church Life – (5) Leadership

1. Michael Green, *Freed to Serve* (London, Hodder & Stoughton, 1988) p 16.
2. Dietrich Bonhoeffer, *The Cost of Discipleship*, op. cit. p 184.
3. Michael Green, *Freed to Serve*, quoted by David Watson in *I Believe In The Church* op. cit. pp 255/6.

Notes 243

4. From an article in *The Times*, Saturday 3 June 1995, entitled 'Church struggles to find a bishop for Winchester'.
5. Donald Coggan, *Sure Foundation* (London, Hodder & Stoughton, 1981). This sermon on Leadership (pp 174–7) was preached at St Paul's Cathedral in November 1979 at a service to commemorate ten great leaders.
6. Ibid.

Chapter 8: Marriage – Made in Heaven

1. Dietrich Bonhoeffer, *The Cost of Discipleship*, op. cit. p 243.
2. In Lawrence J Crabb, *Marriage Builder* (New Malden, Navpress, 1987) the author develops the concept of 'oneness' under the headings 'spirit oneness', 'soul oneness' and 'body oneness'. Those approaching marriage, and those who have been married for years, might benefit from this book, which thoughtfully balances the essential oneness of the married couple with each partner's continuing responsibility to put obeying and honouring God before all else.
3. Howard Guinness, *Sacrifice – A Challenge to Christian Youth* (London, Inter-Varsity Fellowship of Evangelical Unions, 1936) p 31.
4. Lawrence J Crabb, *Marriage Builder*, op. cit, pp 98–99.
5. Dietrich Bonhoeffer, *The Cost of Discipleship*, op. cit. p 243.
6. Donald Coggan, *Sure Foundation*, op. cit. p 229. Extract from a sermon preached to a conference of clergy and lay workers in British Columbia, Canada in September 1978.
7. In quoting this verse, I am not intending to suggest that there is no difference between male and female. That would be to distort it and take it out of context. Gender differences are a fundamental

part of the divine purpose for humanity (Gen 1:27), to be accepted and rejoiced in. Claims for 'equality' which seek to deny this are misdirected. To argue from this that God himself is to be regarded as female is a massive *non-sequitur* and a denial of scriptural revelation. I believe history will show that addressing him as female in worship, and the re-writing of the biblical text to align with currently 'correct' thinking, are an aberration. Attempts to produce, or normalise, individuals who are both physically and psychologically genderless (the subject of a 1995 TV documentary) are morally repugnant. These hard-line statements do not for one moment undermine my assertion that vast and unjustifiable imbalances in the relationships between the sexes have developed down the centuries: much effort is still needed to understand and come to terms with Paul's assertion in Galatians 3:28, and to implement it in the context of our own society.

Chapter 9: Family Life – Training in Discipleship

1. Keith Ward, *The Rule of Love* (London, Daybreak/Darton, Longman and Todd Ltd, 1989) p 8.
2. Ibid.
3. Dietrich Bonhoeffer, *The Cost of Discipleship*, op. cit. p 69.
4. C. S. Lewis, *The Great Divorce* (Glasgow, Collins Fount Paperbacks, 1977) pp 88/9. Of all this remarkable writer's books, this (first published in 1946) is one of the most penetrating, especially in its analysis of the selfishness and selflessness interwoven in all close relationships. I have long struggled to find ways to express the thought that all we love best here will be a part of the joy of heaven, and yet not itself be either the source of our bliss nor the object of our adoration – that the greatest loves of our earthly life

will be enhanced, not reduced, by being subsumed in something altogether greater. Having only recently read *The Great Divorce,* I am greatly relieved to find it all said more convincingly and beautifully than I could ever have hoped to do!
5. See, for example, God's covenant with Abraham, promising blessing to him and 'his descendants after him' (Gen 17:3–8). The idea of passing on the benefit of God's great deeds was central to the institution of the Passover (Ex 12:24–28); brought together later with teaching the family about the blessing of obedience to his laws (Deut 6:4–9; 20–25). Nor is the idea of faith in families/households absent from the New Testament (see, for example, Acts 16:13–15; 31–34).

Chapter 10: Lifestyle and Community

1. Michael Marshall, *The Anglican Church Today and Tomorrow* (London & Oxford, Mowbray, 1984) p 156.
2. From John Keble's hymn 'New every morning is the love,' which can be found in all standard hymn books.
3. This was one of many interesting and surprising facts to emerge from *Faith in the City,* op. cit. See especially paragaphs 2.37 and 7.61–7.65.
4. J.I. Packer, *Laid-Back Religion?* op. cit. pp 56–7. He traces how John Calvin (often cited as the architect of joyless Christianity) and subsequently the Puritans (popularly regarded as professional killjoys) in fact insisted on the sanctity of secular life, thereby breaking the mould of 'evil world' theology which had largely held sway since Augustine. He suggests that it was later generations of Christians – especially in evangelical revivals – who 'bred a narrow and negative other-worldliness', a pietism which 'seldom goes beyond surface-level criticism of the ways of the world'. This has caused many evangelicals (believing they stood

in the traditions of Calvin or the Puritans) to live in the present century with a world-denying rather than a world-affirming outlook which has produced a less positive theology of pleasure than other Christians.
5. Dietrich Bonhoeffer, *The Cost of Discipleship*, op. cit. pp 241/2.
6. Donald Coggan, *Convictions* (London, Hodder & Stoughton, 1975) pp 101–2 (1978 edition).
7. John V Taylor, *Enough is Enough* (London, SCM Press, 1975). This is a seminal book, both for its penetrating analysis of the realities behind the consumer society and its thought-provoking suggestions for a positive, Christian response. A best seller when it appeared, it is unfortunately now out of print.
8. The aims and objectives of the Movement for Christian Democracy are set out in the Westminster Declaration. Copies of this, and further information, can be obtained from MCD, c/o David Alton MP, House of Commons, LONDON, SW1A 0AA (telephone 0171 219 3454).
9. Further information about CARE can be obtained from the CARE Trust, 53 Romney Street, LONDON, SW1P 3RS (telephone 0171 233 0455).
10. Ian Bradley, *The Power of Sacrifice*, op. cit. p 291.
11. For the ideas in this paragraph I am greatly indebted to the final chapter 'Making the sacrifice complete' in Ian Bradley's *The Power of Sacrifice* op. cit.
12. John V Taylor, *Enough is Enough*, op. cit. pp 64–5.
13. Ibid. p 69.
14. Ibid. chapter 4.
15. A versicle and response from one of the services of the Iona Community, published by the Wild Goose Worship Group in *A Wee Worship Book*, op. cit. p 7.
16. John V Taylor, *Enough is Enough*, op. cit. pp 71–2.

17. Dietrich Bonhoeffer, *The Cost of Discipleship*, op. cit. p 31.

Chapter 11: Dying to Self – The Big Issue

1. R. Daly, *The Origins of the Christian Doctrine of Sacrifice* (London, Darton, Longman & Todd, 1978) p 83.
2. Ian Bradley, *The Power of Sacrifice*, op. cit. p 123.
3. Dietrich Bonhoeffer, *The Cost of Discipleship*, op. cit. p 273.
4. For these thoughts I am indebted to Keith Ward, *The Rule of Love*, op. cit. p 123.
5. From a sermon preached in Canterbury Cathedral, reproduced in the *Church of England Newspaper* (date unknown).
6. Bishop Kallistos Ware, *The Orthodox Way* (London, Mowbray, 1979) p 16.
7. Delia Smith, *A Feast for Lent* (London, The Bible Reading Fellowship, 1983) p 58.
8. From an article by E Norman in *The Daily Telegraph*, 2 July 1994, entitled 'Cost of humility'. Quoted by Ian Bradley, *The Power of Sacrifice*, op. cit. p 247.
9. Dietrich Bonhoeffer, *The Cost of Discipleship*, op. cit. pp 42 and 35.
10. Ibid p 273.
11. Nancy Martin, *An Anthology of Prayers for Children and Young People* (London, Hodder & Stoughton, 1975) p 161.
12. Katie B Wilkinson's hymn, written early this century, can be found in most of the newer hymn books, particularly those of an evangelical flavour.